RAILWAYS OF THE
WEST RIDING
OF YORKSHIRE

RAILWAYS OF THE
WEST RIDING OF YORKSHIRE

BERNARD WARR

THE CROWOOD PRESS

First published in 2021 by
The Crowood Press Ltd
Ramsbury, Marlborough
Wiltshire SN8 2HR

enquiries@crowood.com

www.crowood.com

© Bernard Warr 2021

All rights reserved. No part of this publication may be reproduced or transmitted in any form or by any means, electronic or mechanical, including photocopy, recording, or any information storage and retrieval system, without permission in writing from the publishers.

British Library Cataloguing-in-Publication Data
A catalogue record for this book is available from the British Library.

ISBN 978 1 78500 846 7

Publisher's note
Sadly, Bernard Warr passed away shortly after he finished writing this book. We are very grateful to John Hunt and Saskia van Schip for assisting us in bringing the book to publication following his death.

Designed and typeset by Guy Croton Publishing Services,
West Malling, Kent

Cover design by Blue Sunflower Creative

Printed and bound in India by Parksons Graphics Pvt. Ltd., Mumbai.

Contents

Chapter 1:	Introduction	6
Chapter 2:	Railways Around Leeds	16
Chapter 3:	The Influence of York	38
Chapter 4:	The Rise and Rise of Doncaster	58
Chapter 5:	Barnsley and the South Yorkshire Coalfield	66
Chapter 6:	Sheffield and Rotherham	74
Chapter 7:	Airedale and Wharfedale	84
Chapter 8:	The Aire and Calder Watershed	96
Chapter 9:	The Calder Valley	112
Chapter 10:	Huddersfield	132
Abbreviations		142
Index		143

CHAPTER I

Introduction

The West Riding of Yorkshire was one of three historic sub-divisions of the ancient English County of Yorkshire (the others being the North and East Ridings). From 1889 to 1974 it was the administrative county, the County of York, West Riding but was abolished by the Local Government Act 1972 and replaced by the counties of West Yorkshire and South Yorkshire. Over the succeeding thirty years the administrative authority has changed several times but since 2014 it has been two 'combined' authorities, similar in area and function to the two metropolitan counties set up by the 1972 Act. For the purposes of this narration, the term West Riding will be used throughout, unless this conflicts with the actions of successor authorities, in which case the successors will be named.

A Railway Battlefield

That the West Riding has a rich and varied history is beyond doubt. In railway terms, it has been described as the most complex railway network in Britain. It had seven major railway companies with territory in the county and an eighth actively seeking opportunities to gain entry. There were eleven significant joint lines and several minor systems. There appeared to be no overall strategic pattern of territory or route but companies seemed to incessantly vie with one another for supremacy. They pursued major campaigns with many long battles and only co-operated when no alternative existed. In many cases, the justification for competition with another operator for traffic would not stand close scrutiny today. The companies themselves were often woefully inefficient; duplication of facilities was widespread and over twenty-five of the area's towns and villages had two passenger stations, whilst some had three or four!

To seek to understand this railway battlefield it is necessary to look first at what drove the economy of the area. The answer to this lies in the unique physical and economic geography of the region. In the west, and forming a formidable barrier to the neighbouring county of Lancashire, are the Pennine Hills. From north to south these rise steeply from the Lancashire plain and then, in general terms, subside slowly over the territory to the east, until the flat lands of the East Riding are reached. This great Pennine chain is divided by the valleys of seven rivers flowing in an easterly direction: the Swale, Ure, Nidd, Wharfe, Aire, Calder and the Don, all with numerous tributaries. Not to put too fine a point on it, the rivers define Yorkshire, particularly the West Riding. As a means of transport for both raw materials and finished goods they played a pivotal role in facilitating the Industrial Revolution.

> **REMEMBERING THE YORKSHIRE RIVERS**
>
> As a schoolchild, the author clearly remembers being taught the mnemonic SUNWACD (Swale, Ure, Nidd, etc.) as a means of remembering the principal rivers in Yorkshire. Some wag in our number made it easier by simplifying it still further to: 'Sam's uncle never wore any cotton drawers'! Whatever, it worked and sixty years later it is still firmly fixed in the mind.

Before this, it was an area that we would now classify as being of outstanding natural beauty, with dramatic craggy uplands and short, tussocky grass, heather and grey rock mellowing into wooded valley slopes and then rolling green foothills. If such an area existed today it would have been declared a National Park and given the full protection of the law.

Establishment of Trade

As it was, three of its elements were to bring about its industrialization and eventual desecration. The first of these elements was water. Rushing down from the hills in fast-flowing streams, becks and small rivers, the water was soft, lime-free and abundant – ideal for cleansing the wool from the upland sheep. From the thirteenth century, fulling mills had been established in these upland areas to prepare the wool from the sheep for the nearby weavers. Over the next three hundred years, Halifax, Leeds and Wakefield became important centres for woollen cloth. The second element was coal, mined in the area from the twelfth century and becoming a major undertaking for household purposes in Elizabethan times. The final element in the trio was ironstone, excavated from the thirteenth century and smelted with charcoal plundered from the native woodlands to give Sheffield its metal industry, with the abundant water powering the grinding mills and drop forges.

In the Middle Ages, despite the rural nature of the region with its feudal system of employment, trade was established. Agriculture predominated and most people worked on the land. As already referred to, the upland hill farmers were breeding sheep both for meat and their wool. The wool was used to make cloth with domestic-scale weaving looms and the finished products transported by packhorse along the primitive roads to the emergent wool cloth centres of Halifax, Leeds and Wakefield. Although in the Middle Ages sheep farming was confined to the uplands, the success of the cloth trade demanded more and more wool production. This led to lowland pastures, closer to the cloth centres, being turned over to sheep farming. However, by the middle of the eighteenth century, trade was being hindered by the lack of transport capacity to get woollen goods to markets in the UK and to the empire by means of the ports.

Need for Inland Transport

In the late-seventeenth century (1699), the Aire and Calder Navigation, linking Leeds and Wakefield to the sea, was authorized by an Act of Parliament to canalize the River Aire from Leeds and the River Calder from Wakefield, thereby providing a reliable passage by boat to the rivers Ouse and Humber, and thence to the North Sea. The navigation was funded primarily by textile merchants and coal owners who saw better transport infrastructure as a key part of the development of their trade. It was completed by 1704, but took a couple of decades to become established.

The merchants of Huddersfield and Halifax watched the success of the Aire and Calder Navigation and became concerned that the textile industry in their towns would be eclipsed by their rivals in Leeds and Wakefield, who were able to enjoy easy access to markets by using the new navigation system. To rectify this imbalance, they proposed a similar scheme using the rivers Calder and Hebble with appropriate canalized sections on a route from Wakefield to Sowerby Bridge, close to Halifax. Work began in 1758 to make the River Calder navigable above Wakefield, and the whole navigation to Sowerby Bridge was completed in 1770. Sir John Ramsden's Canal, later known as the Huddersfield Broad Canal, was opened in 1776, providing a branch to Huddersfield. Significantly, the Calder and Hebble Navigation, as it became known, was the first waterway to face the engineering challenges and push westwards into the Pennine Hills.

By the 1770s, many of the original waterway promoters had become so wealthy from increased trade that, in addition to purchasing large country estates, they set about promoting further waterway schemes. The impetus for their continued investment came from Yorkshire's traditional rivals west of the Pennines – the county of Lancashire. Here, in 1763, the Duke of Bridgewater, following a visit to the Canal du Midi in France, commissioned a canal from his coal mines in Worsley, to Runcorn via Central Manchester. Overnight the price of coal in the city was halved, an event that was not lost on the thrifty Yorkshiremen in the east.

The Pennines have always formed a major barrier to communication and trade between Lancashire and Yorkshire, particularly in winter. The geography of the Pennines was, therefore, of great importance. Not only were the fells and moors a considerable physical barrier, but their presence influenced the very nature and type of industry and commerce that developed on their flanks. Because of the hills, Lancashire and Yorkshire developed quite distinct economies, with Yorkshire tending to look east and south, and Lancashire turned westwards. Yorkshire had a long and unbroken involvement with woollen textiles, trading originally through London, with the commercial centres of Western Europe. Lancashire, on the other hand, had a textile industry based principally on the linen trade with Ireland. Woollen manufacture was low-key and concerned mainly with serving local markets. To serve the linen trade, there developed, in the eighteenth century, a considerable coastal and international shipping trade, especially with Ireland and the Americas. It was this that provided the most pressing reason for the promotion of the Leeds and Liverpool Canal, since the Bradford wool merchants desperately wanted to have access to the colonial trades working out of Liverpool. This was especially marked when, during the late-eighteenth century, the manufacturers in the Bradford area gradually took over the lucrative worsted industry from its former centre in East Anglia, whilst those in Lancashire expanded by creating an immensely important new textile industry based on cotton, which arrived from America via Liverpool – an industry that was destined, of course, to stimulate and feed a huge explosion of industrial development in Lancashire.

The Coming of the Canals

The Leeds and Liverpool Canal was to play an important role in this Industrial Revolution, long before it was ever thought of as such. Entrepreneurs and merchants on both sides of the Pennines had begun to look at ways of improving inland waterways to move their bulky goods more quickly and cheaply. The canal was the first of the trans-Pennine canals to be started (and the last to be completed). The length and complexity of the route meant that the canal took forty-six years to build and cost five times the original budget.

The Act authorizing the canal was passed in 1770 and, to start with, progress was rapid. By 1773, the lock-free section from Skipton to Bingley was open and, by 1777, the canal between Liverpool, Parbold and Gathurst, near Wigan, and from Leeds to Gargrave, including the branch to Bradford, were all open. However, the high cost of the 'staircase' locks in the Bingley area absorbed all the available funds and work came to a halt. It was to be a further ten years, in 1791, before work re-started on building the canal west from Gargrave. In 1794, a new Act was passed, changing the route to run via Burnley and Blackburn, instead of Whalley and Walton-le-Dale. Foulridge Tunnel was opened in 1796 making the canal navigable from Leeds to Burnley. The section from Burnley to Blackburn took a further fourteen years to construct, and the missing link west of Blackburn to the Lancaster Canal at Johnson's Hillock was not complete until six years later, in 1816, when the canal finally opened as a through route between Liverpool and Leeds. When completed the canal was an enormous 127 miles (204km) long with ninety-one locks rising 487ft (150m) above sea level. Despite the circui-

> **TRAFFIC DELAYS ON THE HUDDERSFIELD NARROW CANAL**
>
> The canal was built for 70ft-long (~21m) narrowboats, whilst the Huddersfield Broad Canal (then called Sir John Ramsden's Canal) could take wider but shorter craft, as used on the Calder and Hebble Navigation. Goods, therefore, had to be trans-shipped between the two at Huddersfield. This enforced double-handling increased costs to unacceptable levels.
>
> To make matters worse, the three-and-a-quarter-mile long (5.25km) Standedge Tunnel was not built wide enough for boats to pass one another. To save money, no towpath was provided, so whilst the horses had the 'luxury' of a walk over Marsden Moor, the boat crew had to propel the boat along by 'legging it' or walking along the tunnel walls whilst lying transversely across the vessel. There were four passing places in the tunnel but, as the traffic increased and with time meaning money for the boat crews, there were frequent fights as crews refused to back off. The Canal Company decided that boats could only be propelled through the tunnel by its own official 'leggers' and to operate a traffic control system. This involved only westbound traffic using the tunnel for a four-hour period, then only eastbound during the next four hours and so on. The tunnel thus became an enormous bottleneck and resulted in processions of boats emerging from the tunnel only to have to queue to use the locks one at a time.

tous route taken, the canal was the most successful long-distance canal in Britain. In 1906, it carried 2,337,401 tons (2,120,000 tonnes) of cargo and was still carrying some commercial traffic in the 1970s.

Meanwhile, frustrated by the slow (and at times non-existent) construction progress of the Leeds and Liverpool Canal, a group of merchants in Ashton, Manchester, sought an Act to construct a new canal from their own Ashton Canal at Dukinfield, eastwards via Stalybridge, Diggle and Marsden to Huddersfield, joining up with the Huddersfield Broad Canal and potentially providing an inland waterway route from the Irish Sea to the North Sea. The Act was passed in 1794 and work began almost immediately.

Despite a length of less than twenty miles (32km), there were numerous engineering difficulties to overcome on the new canal. The construction of Standedge Tunnel – the highest, longest and deepest canal tunnel in Britain – almost bankrupted the entire project with around fifty workers unfortunately losing their lives during its construction. The canal took seventeen years to construct, rather than the planned five. The costs rose to £396,267 (equivalent to £31.7m in 2020), which was more than twice the original budget. Standedge Tunnel alone cost £123,804 (equivalent to £9.9m in 2020) to construct. The result of overspending on this scale meant that shareholders received little or no return on their investment for the next thirty years.

However, despite the construction cost and the navigational difficulties, the canal did enjoy a short period of relative prosperity until 1845, when it was bought by the Huddersfield and Manchester Railway Company.

The Rochdale Canal, the third and final trans-Pennine canal, also obtained its Act of Parliament in 1794. The route was from Sowerby Bridge on the Calder and Hebble Navigation to Castlefield, Manchester, on the Bridgewater Canal, by way of Hebden Bridge and Rochdale, a distance of thirty-two miles (51km) and ninety-two locks. In 1804, it became the first of the three trans-Pennine canals to be fully opened – perhaps due to the choice of a route over the top of the Pennines, avoiding the problems with tunnel construction that had bedevilled the other two waterways. However, the benefit of being without tunnels speeded up construction but left an everlasting legacy of water-supply problems in busy periods. The large number of locks on a relatively short length of canal, which rose to a height of over 600ft (~183m), meant that water supply would always be a problem. Seven reservoirs were built specially to service the canal. Locks were made large enough to accommodate broad-gauge (14ft/~4m) boats with commercial payloads of up to 70 tons (63.5 tonnes). All the locks were given the same fall: meaning that all gates were the same size, making maintenance easier and conserving water by using the same amount of water for each lock operation.

Principal cargoes carried included cotton, wool, coal, limestone, timber, salt, agricultural produce and general merchandise. This canal proved to

INTRODUCTION

Navigable waterways of the West Riding.

be the most successful of the three trans-Pennine routes and for 120 years its shareholders enjoyed a healthy return on their investment (but somewhat diminished at the end of the First World War). From the beginning trade built up steadily, with the highest volume of traffic in 1845, when 979,443 tons (888,536 tonnes) were carried. Even after the canal was leased by the railway companies (1855–76), carryings still amounted to 878,651 tons (797,099 tonnes), all of which was handled profitably

So, by 1820, the canal system was in place and providing the main transport arteries across the West Riding into Lancashire and across to the East Coast. Everything looked set fair for the future prosperity of the canal proprietors. But, within five years a small cloud had appeared on the horizon and, like most small clouds, it could have just melted away

THE STOCKTON AND DARLINGTON RAILWAY COMPANY

Established in the north-east of England, this was the world's first public railway to use steam locomotives. It connected collieries near Shildon with Stockton-on-Tees and Darlington in County Durham, opening on 27 September 1825. Its purpose was to move coal from the mines near Shildon to ships on the River Tees at Stockton and, as noted, was the first to use steam engines. In the early years of the company's existence, these were confined to hauling coal trains, passenger trains being horse drawn until 1833.

The construction of the line was the brainchild of George Stephenson assisted by his son Robert and his elder brother James. Experience gained on this railway put them in the vanguard of railway civil and mechanical engineering, and in the years that followed, their services were much in demand.

and allowed the sun to shine unbroken on the canals and their burgeoning traffic or, as proved to be the case, it could develop into a major storm and threaten the future of the whole system. The small cloud in this case was the railway between Stockton and Darlington.

The Railway Age Begins

Hot on the heels of the Stockton and Darlington Railway, events on the other side of the Pennines drew the attention of the of West Riding businessmen. In the early 1820s, it was felt by their Lancastrian counterparts that the existing means of water transport – the Mersey and Irwell Navigation, the Bridgewater Canal and the Leeds and Liverpool Canal – were making excessive profits from the cotton trade and throttling the growth of Manchester and other towns. A railway between Liverpool and Manchester was proposed to provide a cheap means of transporting both raw materials from the docks and finished goods back to the docks for export. An Act of Parliament was obtained in 1826 and construction began right away, with George Stephenson as engineer.

The directors of the Liverpool and Manchester Railway (L&MR) had originally intended to use stationary steam engines to haul trains along the railway using cables. However, George Stephenson, as their engineer, strongly advocated the use of steam locomotives instead. As the railway was approaching completion, the directors decided to hold a competition to decide whether locomotives could be used to pull the trains and offered a top prize of £500 to the winner; these became known as the Rainhill Trials. A long list of conditions was drawn up and the trials were to last for five days. The length of the L&MR that ran past Rainhill village was straight and level for over 1 mile (1.6km), and was chosen as the site for the trials. Two or three locomotives ran each day with several tests for each locomotive performed over the course of six

The replica of Stephenson's Rocket *seen at Loughborough, Great Central Railway in 2010.*

days. The trials were held before a vast concourse of spectators and the atmosphere was like that of a race meeting. Grandstands were erected alongside the tracks, and between 10,000 and 15,000 people turned up to watch. Bands provided musical entertainment.

The *Rocket*, designed and built by George and Robert Stephenson, was the only locomotive that completed the trials. It averaged 12mph (19km/h) and achieved a top speed of 30mph (48km/h) hauling 13 tons (11.8 tonnes), and was declared the winner of the £500 prize (equal to £43,219 today). The Stephensons were given the contract to produce locomotives for the L&MR.

The Liverpool and Manchester Railway opened on 15 September 1830 and became:

- The world's first inter-city railway.
- The first railway to rely exclusively on locomotives driven by steam power.
- The first to be entirely double-track throughout its length.
- The first to have a signalling system.
- The first to be fully timetabled.
- The first to carry mail.

These developments were not lost on the merchants of the West Riding.

The Leeds and Hull Railway Company was formed in 1824 in Leeds. George Stephenson was appointed as engineer and recommended a double-track railway, operated by locomotives at a speed of 8mph (13km/h). The hills on the route out of Leeds were to have three inclined planes to be worked by three stationary engines. The remainder of the line was to be very nearly level. The company was one of several contemporary projects aimed at linking the east and west sides of northern England, in this case in conjunction with the Manchester and Leeds Railway formed in 1825. Both schemes were not immediately acted upon, in part due to the stock-market crash of 1825, but it has been suggested that the canny Yorkshiremen wanted to see how the Liverpool and Manchester fared before they committed their 'brass'.

The Leeds and Hull scheme stagnated. In the meantime, the Knottingley and Goole Canal (an extension of the Aire and Calder Navigation) opened in 1826, transforming the village of Goole from obscurity into a viable trans-shipment port for Europe. Alarm bells started to ring in Hull.

The growth of Goole as a port to rival Hull was sufficient to spur the Hull-based shareholders of the Leeds and Hull Railway into action. At the end of 1828, they motioned that the railway should be built as far as Selby, with the remainder of the journey to Hull being made by steam packet, most importantly, bypassing Goole. The shareholders passed the proposal at a general meeting in Leeds on 20 March 1829 and the Leeds and Selby Railway Company was formed. Despite strong opposition from the Aire and Calder Navigation, which had a practical monopoly on transportation in the area, a bill was passed in Parliament on 29 May 1830, allowing construction of the line to commence.

By 22 September 1834, a single complete line of track had been built, and the railway was officially opened. A train of ten carriages, hauled by the locomotive Nelson, set out from Marsh Lane Station in Leeds at 6.30am. To the embarrassment of the Leeds and Selby (L&S) directors, and the amusement of the gathered spectators, the locomotive got into difficulty on the incline at the tunnel. The wheels began to slip on wet rails and, despite the application of ash on the rails, initial progress was no better than walking pace. Once the high point of the line was reached, better progress was made:

EFFECT ON WATERWAY DIVIDENDS

The competition for trade brought about by the opening of the Leeds and Selby line, forced the Aire and Calder Navigation to make considerable reductions in their charges and, by implication, dividends paid to shareholders. Previously, that company's monopoly had resulted in enormous dividends, some of over 200 per cent. The competition from the new railway was beginning to bite and waterway proprietors would not see the like of such dividends again.

FINDING A LEADER – GEORGE HUDSON

Born in 1800 to John and Elizabeth Hudson, George Hudson was unfortunately orphaned at the age of eight and seems to have been brought up by his elder brothers, William and John. He left school at the age of fifteen and was apprenticed to Bell and Nicholson, a firm of drapers in College Street, York. He must have shown great promise during his apprenticeship, which he finished in 1820, as he was taken on as a tradesman and given a share in the business early in 1821. On 17 July that year he married Nicholson's daughter Elizabeth and the cynics amongst us might conclude that this union had some influence on his success. When Bell retired, the firm became Nicholson and Hudson. George soon repaid the faith his father-in-law had shown in him by developing the company, which, by 1827, was the largest drapery and, indeed, the largest business in York. In the same year, his great-uncle Matthew Botrill fell ill and Hudson attended at his bedside. In thanks for this, the old man made a will leaving him his fortune of £30,000.

at Garforth, on a stretch of track falling 1 in 180, a speed of 20mph (32km/h) was attained. Selby was reached before 9am. The return journey took one hour and sixteen minutes. The following day, the 23rd, two trains were run each way, with a better timing of sixty-five minutes from Leeds to Selby.

Both lines of track were complete by 15 December 1834, when the railway began to take goods traffic. Although passengers were accommodated (in goods wagons), the company's focus was on freight and used its line as a feeder for waterborne transport after trans-shipment at Selby.

The merchants and the manufacturers of the West Riding, having seen the success of the first intercity railway, the Liverpool and Manchester and, in 1833, the passing of Acts of Parliament for lines to London from Lancashire, realized that they would be at a commercial disadvantage unless they acted quickly to facilitate similar transport facilities for their own area.

The merchants of the West Riding needed to find someone with vision and drive who could see the 'bigger picture' and lead others of like mind, but who were perhaps less visionary, in the ways of this new railway business. There is an old adage 'cometh the hour, cometh the man', and this was demonstrably true in the early 1830s when a man with no background in transport came on the scene who was to have enormous influence on railway development in the West Riding and beyond, earning himself the title 'The Railway King'. This was, of course, George Hudson. Hudson had, as we have seen, no former interest in railways but, seeing them as a potentially profitable investment, he arranged a public meeting in 1833 to discuss building a line from York to Leeds. Resulting from this meeting, a group of York businessmen formed a railway committee. The initial idea was to link York to Leeds to enable the city to enjoy cheaper coal and emulate the industrial success being enjoyed by Leeds, Bradford and other West Riding towns. Hudson was treasurer of this group and subsequently subscribed for 500 shares, becoming the largest shareholder. They retained John Rennie to survey the line and Hudson accompanied him, learning the practicalities of railway construction and of dealing with landowners.

Disappointingly, despite the success of the locomotive-powered Liverpool and Manchester Railway on the other side of the Pennines, Rennie produced plans for a horse-drawn line (in 1834) and matters fell into abeyance. Later in the same year, Hudson met George Stephenson by chance in Whitby, they became friends and business associates. He learnt of Stephenson's dream of a railway from London, using the London and Birmingham Railway from Rugby, through Derby and Leeds to Newcastle – but (to Hudson's dismay) bypassing York. Later that year, at a public meeting in York, the York and North Midland Railway (Y&NMR) was formed to build a railway line to a junction with the proposed North Midland Railway near Normanton. While the Y&NMR route was being planned, the North Midland Railway (NMR) was formed (in 1835) to build the line from Derby to Leeds. This would connect with the Midland Counties Railway (MCR) at Derby and, therefore, via the London and Birmingham Railway, provide rail access to London.

The Y&NMR received its Act of Parliament on 21 June 1836. At its first official meeting, Hudson was elected chairman with other officers, including James Meek, James Richardson and Richard Nichol-

INTRODUCTION

Hebden Bridge railway station seen in October 2010. Note the staggered platforms.

son (Hudson's brother-in-law). George Stephenson was appointed engineer for the line, a private bill was presented to Parliament seeking permission to build the railway and Royal Assent was given on 21 June 1836 to the Act that confirmed Hudson as chairman.

The first railway to connect the West Riding with Lancashire was the Manchester and Leeds Railway Company. Plans to form such a company had been around since 1825, but obtaining the necessary Act of Parliament proved elusive. It was not until July 1836 that the Act received the Royal Assent and construction could begin. In order to overcome the challenge of the Pennines, Stephenson took a circuitous route from Manchester through Rochdale to Littleborough, where a 1.6-mile tunnel (2.6km), aptly named Summit Tunnel, saw the beginning of the descent, continuing the line through Walsden and Todmorden into the Upper Colne Valley. From there the line meandered on through Hebden Bridge, Sowerby Bridge and Horbury to join the existing NMR at Normanton to reach Leeds.

The choice of route meant that the line bypassed the important trade centres of Oldham, Halifax, Huddersfield and Bradford – something the company would come to regret in future years.

The company had given an undertaking to construct a branch line from their main line at Cooper Bridge to Huddersfield after the backers of the Huddersfield and Leeds Railway had withdrawn their competing scheme in early 1836. However, their proposal for a low-level line along the Calder Valley limited the potential for connecting to other routes and received little support at meetings held in Huddersfield in 1844. Instead, the high-level line proposed by the Huddersfield and Manchester Railway and Canal Company was viewed more favourably and was approved by Parliament in April 1845.

Not to be outdone by their fellow Yorkshiremen in Leeds, the merchants of Sheffield could see advantage to their trade with better communications. The canal route to Manchester and Liverpool involved a long northwards detour through the Pennines, a journey taking eight days, with the more arduous direct route by horse and cart taking about two days

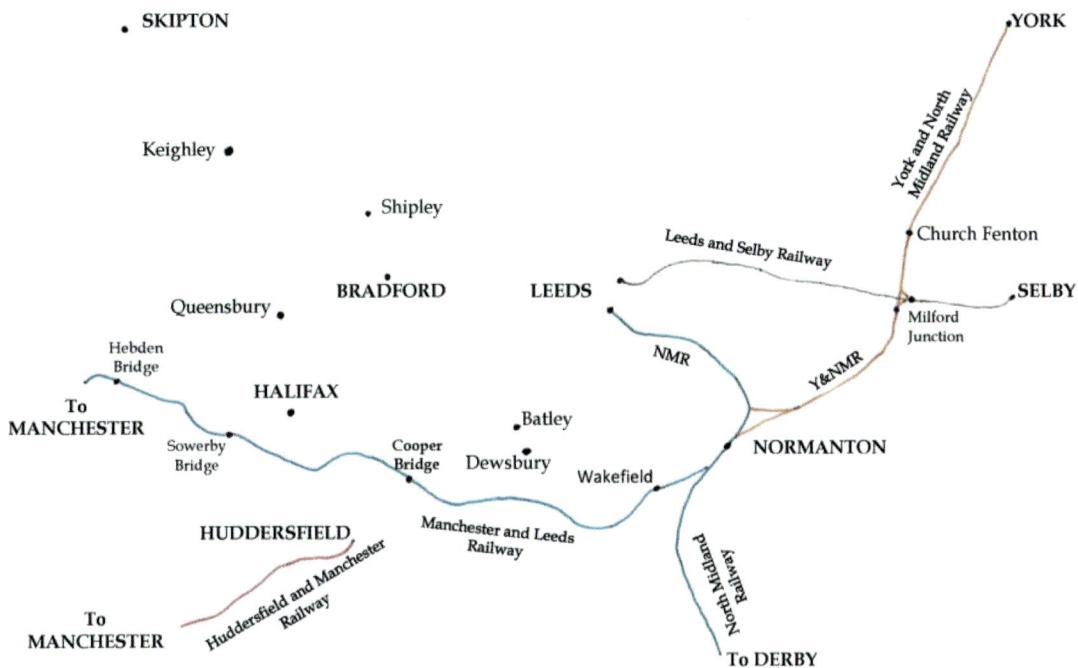

West Riding Railways 1845.

but with much smaller loads. Proposals for a railway via Whaley Bridge and the Hope Valley led to the formation of a 'Sheffield and Manchester Railway' with a prospectus issued in 1830. Concerns were expressed at the severity of the gradients and an alternate route via Penistone was put forward. The proprietors of the company could not make up their minds as to which route to select and this indecisiveness led to a waning of public interest, resulting in the proposal being dropped.

However, the apparent success of the Liverpool and Manchester Railway revived interest and, in 1835, Charles Vignoles was asked to examine another route going via Woodhead and Penistone. A new company, the 'Sheffield, Ashton-under-Lyne and Manchester Railway' was formed. The new line could be worked by adhesion and required only a 2-mile (3km) tunnel. Vignoles and Joseph Locke were asked to make independent surveys and, in October, met to reconcile any differences, at which time they decided that a longer tunnel would reduce the gradients involved. The line obtained its Act of Incorporation in Parliament on 5 May 1837. Construction began quickly but the tunnelling was arduous and, although sections of the line opened earlier, the whole route did not open for business until 1845.

In the few short years between 1830 and 1845, the basic structure of railways in the West Riding was complete. Railways had been authorized in an east-to-west direction, giving access from Leeds to Manchester and Liverpool; from north to south, connecting York with Leeds via Normanton, south to Derby and on to London by means of the Midland Counties and Grand Junction Railway Companies, and in the south of the county, Sheffield was connected to Manchester via the Woodhead route. What happened next became almost unbelievable as 'railway mania' gripped the country. Railways were proposed the length and breadth of the kingdom, and none more so than in Yorkshire. The plan 'West Riding Railways 1845' shows railways open or under construction in 1845, forming the basis of the 'railway battleground' that was to be fought over so wastefully in the coming decades.

CHAPTER 2

Railways Around Leeds

We have already seen how the merchants of Leeds had their town in the vanguard of West Yorkshire railway development. However, railways – or more accurately wagonways – had been established much earlier in the area in 1755.

The Aire and Calder Navigation, opened in 1704, gave access to the sea by means of the Ouse and the Humber. There was an abundance of coal within a few miles of the Navigation and the combination of the availability of waterborne transport and the vast coal reserves led to many collieries being developed. The difficulty was transporting the freshly mined coal from pit to barge. The only option was by horse and cart, which was slow and expensive.

The Yorkshire Wagonways

Further north, at about the same time, wagonways were being established and were flourishing in the Northumberland and Durham coalfields. The coal wagons had flangeless wooden rollers that ran on wooden rails supported by transverse timbers spaced out at approximately 2ft (0.6m). Each wooden rail had an upright timber to guide the roller along the rail. Gravity and horses aided the wagon to descend from pit to staithe (quay), and the horses were used to bring the empty wagons back to the pit. By the middle years of the eighteenth century, wagonways had become an integral part of the transport of coal away from the coalfields of the North-East.

A prominent North-Eastern mine owner was Charles Brandling of Gosforth Hall, Killingworth, near Newcastle. He inherited estates and collieries at Middleton, near Leeds, in 1849 and was immediately critical of the methods used to get the coal to the Navigation, meaning, in effect, that it was costing him more than his competitor, the Fentons of Rothwell, who used the river for transport directly into Leeds. Brandling, through his agent, Richard Humble (also from Tyneside), built a wagonway from Middleton to Thwaite Gate on the River Aire, which is believed to have been operational by 1755. Brandling soon realized that if the wagonway went into the centre of Leeds, he could avoid paying dues to the Navigation proprietors altogether. He negotiated wayleaves with the landowners but, just to be sure, he obtained an Act of Parliament dated 9 June 1758 to give validity to these agreements. This became the first Act of Parliament authorizing a railway. The gauge was 4ft 1in (1.25m) and was double-tracked so that loaded wagons could easily pass the returning empties without 'let or hindrance'. The route was from Middleton to Casson Close, Leeds, near Meadow Lane on the River Aire. Charles Brandling could supply coal at very favourable prices

> **INFLUENCES ON THE MIDDLETON RAILWAY**
>
> International affairs, in the form of the Napoleonic wars (1803–15), next had an influence on the fortunes of the Middleton undertaking. The demand for horses for military use inflated their price almost beyond recognition. As a way of alleviating this cost, John Blenkinsop, the agent appointed in 1808, looked seriously at the new steam engines that were being trialled elsewhere, but found that they played havoc with the cast-iron rails then in use, causing regular breakages. He had an idea for a kind of rack railway and, with the help of Matthew Murray, developed and patented his own unique system.
>
> Murray was a gifted and inventive engineer who learned his trade making specialized machinery for flax spinning in Darlington. A downturn in the flax trade in 1789 led him (reputedly) 'to walk to Leeds with his bag of tools on his back'. He quickly established himself and became a founding director of Fenton, Murray and Wood of the Round Forge. Before his involvement with the Middleton Railway, at Murray's instigation, Fenton, Murray and Wood were involved in designing and constructing steam engines. It is not surprising then, that as part of his remit from Blenkinsop, he also supplied engines to the railway. The first of these, believed to be *Salamanca*, came into use in 1812 and was an immediate success. Blenkinsop claimed that each engine replaced fourteen horses, could haul twenty-seven wagons at 3½mph (5.6km/h) on the level and reduced costs. Two similar engines were purchased the following year, allowing coal production to soar. In 1814, coal output reached a record 100,000 tons (91,000 tonnes).

and through this 'cut-throat' competition became the sole supplier of coal to Leeds. This, together with the opening of the Leeds and Liverpool Canal as far as Skipton in 1777, facilitated the Industrial Revolution in the city. Cheap Middleton coal gradually enabled Leeds to become a centre for the many developing industries that used coal as a source of heat, including pottery, brick and glass-making, metal-working, brewing or as a source of power for mill and factory engines.

Although in a semi-monopoly position, Brandling was constantly having to ward off competition. In 1789, Beeston New Colliery was joined to the wagonway making a total length of about four-and-a-quarter miles (6.8km). In the last thirty years of the eighteenth century, the population of Leeds almost doubled to about 31,000 and the quantity of coal supplied rose to about 50,000 tons (~45,000 tonnes). As was to be expected, this heavy use of the wooden rails led to rapid wear. To counter this, hard cast-iron plates (a very new material then) were laid on the rails.

There were some early successes with West Riding-built steam engines, but these were eclipsed by the opening of the Stockton and Darlington Railway in 1825 and the Liverpool and Manchester in 1830. Brandling's collieries were suffering from increasing competition and, in 1834, they passed into the hands of trustees. The hard-worked steam engines were, after more than twenty years' work, ready for replacement, but a fall in the price of fodder and a good supply of horses allowed horse traction to be reinstated from 1835 instead.

In 1862, the Brandling estates were sold and steam traction was reinstated. In 1881, the gauge was converted to standard gauge but the railway slowly contracted and, by 1958, there were plans to close it completely. However, the Middleton Railway again made history by being the first railway in the country to be taken over and run by volunteers from June 1960.

The Middleton Railway was a freight railway and, understandably, never seems to have aspired to cater for passengers in its early years. This was not the case with the Leeds and Selby Railway, which carried passengers from the beginning.

Passenger-Carrying Railways

The original Leeds and Selby proposal, in about 1824, was for a railway from Leeds to Hull to connect with a proposed Leeds to Manchester line. As we have seen in Chapter 1, neither scheme was proceeded with initially, but the opening of the Knottingley and Goole Canal, as an extension of the Aire and Calder Navigation, caused considerable disquiet in Hull where merchants had visions of the once obscure village of Goole overtaking Hull as an ideal trans-shipment port for European trade over the North Sea. At a meeting in Leeds on 20 March 1829, the shareholders of Leeds and Hull Railway Company resolved to shorten their plans to construct a rail-

Between the Marsh Lane terminus of the Leeds and Selby Railway and the 1899-built Neville Hill Depot, lies Park Road cutting. In this late 1960s view, an unidentified BR Class 37 passes with an empty stock working. JOHN HUNT

The Leeds and Selby Railway became part of the York and North Midland in 1845 and by 1854, the North Eastern Railway. The NER built a new locomotive shed at Selby, just south-west of the station in 1871, remaining in use until 1959. This view, taken sometime between 1957 and the shed closure in 1959, shows two NER stalwarts: T1 4-8-0T, 69912 dating from 1909 and J27 0-6-0 65793 dating from 1906.

way to Selby only, where a packet boat connection to Hull would be made. The company was renamed the Leeds and Selby Railway Company (L&SR). The route was resurveyed and placed before Parliament. Despite strong opposition from the Aire and Calder Navigation, which had a practical monopoly on transportation in the area, a bill was passed in Parliament on 29 May 1830 allowing construction of the line.

The Marsh Lane terminus in Leeds and the station at Selby were early examples of what would become 'railway architecture': both were long, rectangular sheds, with wooden-trussed roofs, supported internally on cast-iron columns. The stations served for both passenger and freight, with additional tracks external to the sheds for coal; there was no platform for passengers. Both stations had coal depots and the Leeds Station contained the facilities for maintenance of engines and wagons. The rear of the Selby station backed on to the Ouse, across a road (Ousegate) from jetties that would allow a continuation of the journey to Hull by packet boat. The continuation of the railway toward Hull, replacing the steam-packet services, was not completed until 1840.

The line to Selby was completed by December 1834 and services commenced immediately, with the L&SR becoming the first main-line railway in Yorkshire. Surprisingly, the undertaking was not the financial success that would have been expected. After six years, although in profit, the average dividend on a £100 share over the period 1837 to 1840 was a meagre one pound, sixteen shillings and nine pence (£1.84). However, the L&SR offered a direct route into Leeds from the east. The acquisitive Y&NMR recognized this and leased the whole L&SR on 9 November 1840 for £17,000 per annum.

The Y&NMR's first act was to close the L&S line to passengers, west of Milford through to Leeds. So, despite the Y&NMR line being 4 miles (6.5km) longer, passengers now had no choice but to use it. In 1848, the line west of Milford was closed to freight as well; Marsh Lane Station was at that time still a terminus and so useless for through traffic to Manchester and beyond. Passenger services were reinstated in 1850, but freight continued to run to Leeds via Castleford and not Marsh Lane. In 1844, the Y&NMR obtained an Act of Parliament for it to absorb the L&SR entirely, with the result that the L&SR, as an independent entity, ceased to exist.

In the period 1835–37, a wave of new railway company promotions contributed to the development of Leeds as a regional centre. The North Midland Railway from Derby and the Manchester and Leeds Railway approaching along the Calder Valley, both shared the services of George Stephenson as their engineer. Stephenson had a cherished concept that main-line railways should minimize the gradients of their lines, ideally no steeper than 1 in 330, even if that increased the distance (and, therefore, cost) and avoided intermediate population centres. Following this concept, Stephenson took the Manchester and Leeds on a northerly route through Rochdale, crossed the Pennines at Littleborough through the Summit Tunnel and then followed the Calder Valley through Walsden and Todmorden, meandering on through Hebden Bridge, Sowerby Bridge and Horbury, to join the North Midland Railway at Normanton to reach Leeds, Hunslet Lane. This route was almost 62 miles (99km) between its two termini, which compared unfavourably with the direct route distance of 40 miles (64km). Additionally, it carefully bypassed the important trade centres of Oldham, Halifax, Huddersfield and Bradford. Despite having relegated itself to the 'second tier' of trans-Pennine railways by these early routing decisions, the Manchester and Leeds Railway successfully commenced running on 1 March 1841.

With the arrival of these railway lines in Leeds it would have been logical for one of them to extend northwards toward Newcastle, with Leeds at the centre of an east–west route (Liverpool to Hull) and a north–south route from London to Newcastle. However, the logic of this last route was frustrated by George Hudson's ambition to make York the railway centre of the north. He prevailed upon the Great North of England Railway, which was then promoting a line to link Newcastle to both Leeds and York, to concentrate exclusively on York.

With three railway companies' lines converging on Normanton, it was bound to be a busy place! This view shows the multiplicity of lines north of the station (which is behind the camera) and looks down into the engine sheds, first opened by the NER in 1875. Note the massive coaling plant in the centre of the picture. Although the shed had been ceded to BR by the LNER in 1948, at the time of this photograph (July 1965), the locomotive allocation was down to twenty-five engines, mostly WD 2-8-0s and some former LMSR types, demonstrating the depot's main work: hauling heavy mineral trains. JOHN HUNT

Hudson's grip on the railway development around Leeds intensified with his decision to close the Leeds and Selby between Leeds and Milford Junction already mentioned. Traffic on the Y&NMR route became hopelessly congested and sometimes could take two hours to get from Leeds to York. Passengers for Hull did not fare any better, and tales of long waits for a connection on the bleak and windswept Milford platform abounded.

The North Midland Railway was also beset by problems. Stephenson had pursued his original concept and would not accept any gradient steeper than 1 in 130 and curves of less than 1-mile radius (1.6km). Where possible, he followed the river valleys all the way from Derby to Masborough (where a junction with the Sheffield and Rotherham Railway was made) and on to Normanton and Castleford to Leeds. The civil engineering was on a massive scale. Major bridges were at Oakenshaw, over the Barnsley Canal, and the Calder and Chevet Viaducts. In addition, there were massive stone-retaining walls for the cutting through Belper and the embankment north of Ambergate. Although the general radius of curves was 1 mile (1.6 km), gradients were steep and practically the whole length was embanked or in cuttings, when not proceeding through a tunnel. The number of men employed was 8,600, with eighteen pumping engines providing drainage. It was tough work and many lives were lost, particularly in the boring of the Clay Cross Tunnel.

The line opened on 11 May 1840 to Masborough and through to Leeds on 1 July. The line enjoyed only limited financial success due to the high cost of construction brought about by Stephenson's self-imposed limits on gradient and curvature, the terrain through which the line was constructed and the extravagant design of stations and other buildings. Moreover, by the time it opened, the country had entered an economic depression. In the first two years of operation, dividends were as low as 3.5 per cent where investors had been promised double-digit returns. The management introduced economies but, in 1842, the dividend was a mere 1 per cent and the influential Lancashire and Yorkshire shareholders called for a Committee of Enquiry. This was agreed and the membership included George Hudson, who, after a tour of the complete network, insisted on drastic measures. Against the wishes of the Derby directors, Hudson and the others insisted on halving expenditure. At a meeting on 16 November 1842 in Leeds, the Lancashire and Yorkshire shareholders had their way and the economies called for by Hudson were agreed. Shortly afterwards, at a meeting in Derby on 30 November 1842, six directors resigned and were replaced by George Hudson and his fellow shareholders.

One of the first acts of the new directors was to close Beighton, Killamarsh and Kilnhurst stations from 1 January 1843. Boys, instead of men, would work points at junctions, services were reduced, fares were raised and several carriages were sold. A quarter of the footplate staff was sacked. The remainder protested over the lower wages and were sacked as well, without pay in lieu of notice on Christmas Eve 1842. Hudson employed in their place enginemen he described as 'skilled replacements', who included in their number a platelayer, a fireman and a stonemason, two of whom had been sacked for drunkenness and one who had been sacked for overturning a train of wagons.

The result was chaos, with trains running late or erratically and the remainder of the workforce demoralized. Finally, a passenger was killed when a luggage train, allegedly being driven by the fireman with only three weeks' driving experience, collided with the rear of a stationary train at Cudworth in fog on 12 January 1843. The inquest into the death of the passenger criticized the cutbacks and sent the 24-year-old driver, Edward Jenkins, to the York Assizes for trial on a charge of manslaughter. The jury at the trial acquitted Jenkins and censured the directors. There was widespread publicity about the trial and after the verdict had been reached, the NMR suddenly found, deservedly, that it had gained a reputation for being the most dangerous railway in the land. The reputational damage to the commercial prospects that this brought to the North Midland was not lost on Hudson and he set about finding a solution. In the short term, some of the economies introduced were rescinded, but not before the Board of Trade had severely criticized the company.

The performance problems faced by Hudson with the NMR were compounded south of Derby by the strong competition between the Birmingham and Derby Junction Railway (B&DJR) and the MCR for transport, particularly of coal, to London, which almost drove both out of business. The B&DJR offered a time from Derby to London of around seven hours, but when the MCR began operating, it could make the journey in an hour less. The B&DJR lowered its fares but this simply resulted in a price war. The situation between the two railways was becoming steadily worse. Hudson's first approach was to the Midland Counties in 1843 and he suggested an amalgamation of the three companies. All three lines were in dire straits and paying minuscule dividends. However, the MCR rebutted his suggestion of the triple merger and he was forced to re-think his plans. His next move was to successfully negotiate in secret with the B&DJR to amalgamate with the NMR, which would remove all the MCR's trade from Derby and the north. When news leaked out, shares in the B&DJR rose dramatically.

In August 1843, he returned to the MCR's board of directors with an ultimatum and he persuaded the MCR's shareholders to override their board. Finally, on 22 September 1843, at a meeting in Derby, the triple merger was agreed. In 1844, the Birmingham and Derby Junction Railway, the Midland Counties and the North Midland Railway merged to form the new Midland Railway.

A line from Leeds to Bradford had been proposed as early as 1830, but it is worth taking a moment to consider transport history in the area before that momentous date.

During the early eighteenth century, Bradford had become an important centre of the wool trade, but was beginning to be hampered by the cost of transport – the town is not on a river of any size and lies in a deep valley. During the 1760s and 1770s, a group of Bradford businessmen were the driving force behind the creation of the Leeds and Liverpool Canal and its offshoot the Bradford Canal, in order to improve the town's communications. The canals were very successful for Bradford but, from the 1830s, railways began to be built around the country and, again, a group of Bradford businessmen were eager to benefit from this development. Various schemes were started, but none received enough support. Nor could the North Midland Railway be persuaded to extend its Derby to Leeds line to Bradford.

At last, in 1843, they succeeded in forming the Leeds and Bradford Railway (L&BR) Company, with George Hudson as chairman. They obtained the necessary Act of Parliament in July 1843, to build a line from Wellington Street, Leeds, to Bradford via Shipley, and also a link to the North Midland Railway's terminus at Hunslet Lane, to allow connections to the south. The line opened on 1 July 1846. The Wellington Street terminus in Leeds was much more central than Marsh Lane or Hunslet Lane, and the opening of the L&BR extension to this latter station did away with much of its passenger traffic.

Not surprisingly, the engineer in charge of the project was George Stephenson. He routed the line up the Aire valley to Shipley, and then south up the Bradford Dale to Bradford – the only reasonably flat approach to the town.

With Hudson involved in both the L&BR and the Midland Companies, the Midland was inevitably closely associated with the L&BR from the start, but they remained separate entities for several years. However, by 1853 the Midland had absorbed the L&BR.

The potential further development of the L&BR was soon realized and a new Act of Parliament, 'The Leeds and Bradford (Shipley–Colne Extension) Railway Act 1845', was authorized on 30 June of that year, empowering the company to build its line as an extension of the L&BR, which was still under construction. In July 1846, this new company was also leased to the Midland Railway, which later absorbed it on 24 July 1851.

The line was opened in sections, with Skipton being reached on 7 September 1847, initially as a single track, but doubled by the end of the year. Trains ran between Bradford and Skipton; passengers to and from Leeds changed at Shipley.

The final section between Skipton and Colne was contracted on 9 September 1846 and opened on 2 October 1848. At Colne it made an end-on junction with the East Lancashire Railway's Blackburn, Burnley, Accrington and Colne Extension Railway, which did not open until 1 February 1849. By 2 April of the same year, the line was part of a through route between Leeds and Liverpool, becoming the fourth trans-Pennine route, although most passenger trains were local between Skipton and Colne.

Conflict and Upheaval

The Ingleton branch is an example of conflict in the northern Pennine hills. Battlelines were drawn between the ruthless giant of the London and North Western Railway (L&NWR) and its challenger, the ambitious Midland. Each operated a station at Ingleton, either side of the valley, with a sandstone viaduct of eleven arches spanning the divide between them. It carried the contentious route from Clapham to Lowgill 80ft (24m) over the River Greta. Built as an express link between the West Riding and Scotland, the line spent a hundred years as a quiet, rural backwater, its relegation caused by corporate squabbling. The story of the Ingleton Branch is one of unrealized potential.

In February 1845, the North Western Railway

The Ingleton branch.

Company issued a prospectus for four sections of new line, connecting the Leeds and Bradford Railway's extension at Skipton with the Lancaster and Carlisle Railway. The plans, drawn up by Charles Vignoles and Robert Stephenson, featured a branch to a northerly junction near Lowgill, thus creating the shortest route from London to Scotland.

Two of the proposals had been jettisoned by the time Royal Assent was granted in June 1846, meaning that the branch had now become the main line. Its first sod was cut six months later and construction work soon began at Ingleton.

But the chill wind of financial frugality was beginning to blow. Daunting engineering requirements at the northern end of the line threatened to suck £350,000 from the company's coffers, so attention was refocused on the simpler second scheme, from a junction at Clapham to Lancaster.

The foundations of the viaduct – complete but redundant – stretched out beyond the buffer stops at Ingleton's single-line terminus. The first passengers arrived from Skipton on 30 July 1849 but, within a year, the Lancaster spur opened and the Clapham–Ingleton section was abandoned – probably the shortest-lived train service in railway history!

Despite its strategic significance, the missing link to Lowgill valiantly withstood all efforts to resurrect it. Five companies played roles in a complex plot of dithering and brinkmanship until, in June 1857, a Commons Committee accepted proposals from the Lancaster and Carlisle Railway. The builders moved in during the summer of 1858. Its 19 miles (30km) were split into four contractual sections, three of which encompassed substantial viaducts: Lowgill, Lune and Ingleton, the last being the longest at 800ft (240m). Forty men were engaged to build it and did so, without loss of life or broken limb, in just two years.

This ordered progress on the ground was set against a background of upheaval in the boardroom. The Lancaster and Carlisle Railway, including the Ingleton Branch, was leased to the all-conquering L&NWR. Meantime, the North Western Railway had been swallowed up by the Midland, which set about doubling the single line into Ingleton, anticipating completion of the new link through to Scotland. The trouble was that these two giants held a mutual animosity, as the Midland had got into bed with the Great Northern Railway – the L&NWR's leading competitor – to gain access into London.

Ingleton was reborn, but found itself on the frontline when its inaugural train pulled in on Monday 16 September 1861. Unable to reach agreement for shared use of the Midland Station, the L&NWR opened its own at the northern end of the viaduct, about a mile out of town. Thus, passengers were confronted by a strenuous hike when changing trains, particularly if burdened by luggage.

Services on the branch were slow – taking an hour from one end to the other – and the L&NWR deliberately mistimed its trains to ensure poor connections with the Midland. The promised through services didn't materialize.

These antics infuriated both passengers and operators alike. With complaints mounting, the Midland contemplated a retreat from the Ingleton Branch to engineer its own route through to Carlisle. Faced with the prospect of competition for its Scottish traffic, the L&NWR was immediately overwhelmed by a breath of common sense and sought a more cooperative future. The rivals spent months at the negotiating table but, on the brink of an accord, the Midland withdrew in a dispute over rights at Carlisle.

In August 1865, planning got underway on the Midland's independent line from Settle, navigating a stormy Parliamentary passage to receive Royal Assent a year later. Undeterred, the L&NWR made more conciliatory noises and a deal was finally done to allow the Midland running powers over its route north. But the politicians were unimpressed and rejected the Midland's application to abandon the Settle–Carlisle scheme. For the Ingleton Branch, this effectively killed off any lingering aspirations of main-line status.

With its future clear, the frosty relationship between the competing companies began to thaw a little. L&NWR's trains were soon running through to Ingleton's Midland Station, although the continued operation of two halts in the town proved bewildering for some passengers, uncertain where to board their train. For a penny, trippers could take a ride between the two and enjoy the vista from the viaduct.

Shifting Trade and Personnel

The concentration of new railway development around Leeds brought about a change of emphasis in the nature of trade. From about 1837, the traditional cloth trade was starting to decline because of competition from other parts of the West Riding, particularly Bradford. Fortunately, this was more

In May 1975, former Lambton, Hetton and Joicey Collieries (LH&JC) No 29, a Kitson 0-6-2 of 1904, arrives at Goathland Station on the North York Moors Railway, having just ascended the 1 in 49 gradient up from Grosmont.

than offset by a rapid growth of engineering industries, many to do with the new railways.

Kitson and Company was started in 1835 by James Kitson at the Airedale Foundry off Pearson Street, Hunslet, with Charles Todd as a partner. Todd had been apprenticed to Matthew Murray at the Round Foundry in Holbeck, Leeds. Initially, the firm made parts for other builders until it was joined, in 1838, by David Laird, a wealthy farmer who was looking for investments, and the company became Todd, Kitson and Laird. That year saw the production of the company's first complete locomotives, for the Liverpool and Manchester Railway. However, Todd left almost immediately and the company was known variously as Kitson and Laird, or Laird and Kitson. The order for six engines for the Liverpool and Manchester began with 0-4-2 *Lion*. Around 1858, it was withdrawn from service and sold to the Mersey Docks and Harbour Board, where it was jacked-up off its wheels and used for pumping water. In 1930 it was restored and remains in preservation at The Great Port Gallery at the Museum of Liverpool. In 1953, *Lion* starred in the Ealing Comedies film *The Titfield Thunderbolt*.

In 1842, Laird, who was not receiving the financial return he expected, left the partnership. James Kitson was then joined by Isaac Thompson and William Hewitson and the company becoming Kitson, Thompson and Hewitson. In 1851, the company exhibited an early tank locomotive at the Great Exhibition and was awarded a gold medal. In 1858, Thompson left and the firm became Kitson and Hewitson, then, finally, Kitson and Company in 1863 when Hewitson died.

The company became very successful and built locomotives for many British railways, including the Midland Railway, the Lancashire and Yorkshire Railway, and the South Eastern Railway. The company had customers worldwide and, from 1855, many Indian railways became major customers. From 1866, the company produced a large proportion of the Midland Railway double-framed goods engines designed by Matthew Kirtley and, from 1869, began building a series of engines for Russia. In all, about 5,400 locomotives were built over a period of 101 years. At least ten have survived into preservation, with probably the best known being the Lambton, Hetton and Joicey Collieries No 29 (Kitson No 4263), an 0-6-2 built in 1904 and recently returned to service on the North Yorkshire Moors Railway.

Mention has already been made of Fenton, Murray and Jackson (née Wood) in connection with the Middleton Railway, who were very early builders of steam engines. This company probably reached its greatest heights when the Great Western Railway placed an order for twenty 7ft single Firefly-class locomotives in 1840. The boom in railway equipment production subsided a little in the early 1840s, but it was soon to accelerate into a further 'boom' period from 1844.

The establishment of these companies to serve the demand for railway equipment brought about an upsurge in population to meet the jobs that were created. This upsurge was not confined to the railway industry alone and there was a similar increase in activity in commercial services, marketing and the retail sector. Population of the city rose to over 150,000 by 1841 and 172,000 by 1851. Despite these apparent 'boom' times, Leeds suffered something of a depression in the late 1830s and early 1840s. However, by the mid-1840s, the return on investments in railway companies rose at an incredible rate, reaching over 6 per cent from a base of 2–3 per cent a few years earlier. The railway mania had begun and commercial activity in the city rose to new heights.

Two other railway companies with an interest in Leeds were granted Parliamentary approval during the period of the railway mania. The first of these was the Leeds and Thirsk Railway, which received permission for a line from Leeds to Thirsk on 21 July 1845, with construction starting on 20 October 1845. Extension of the line into Leeds was delayed by problems encountered during the construction of the 3,761yd (3,439km) long Bramhope Tunnel. The contractor encountered large quantities of water that had to be pumped out and many workers

---

THE WEST RIDING UNION RAILWAY

Like all stock-market surges, the railway mania of 1843 to 1845 was more concerned with buying and selling railway company shares than with improving the commercial services provided by the companies. Nevertheless, in the quest for ever better returns, all manner of lines were promoted to serve Leeds, but only four managed to be authorized by Parliament. These included the Leeds, Dewsbury and Manchester Railway of 1845, which was promoted with the Huddersfield and Manchester Railway and Canal Company, the two systems providing a very direct link between Manchester and Leeds, and managing to serve two important West Riding towns en route (these being Dewsbury and Huddersfield). Similarly, seeking to improve the travellers' lot between Leeds and Manchester was the West Riding Union Railway (WRUR) of August 1846. A clause in its act of incorporation required it to merge with the Manchester and Leeds Railway, which it did in November 1846. The proposal was for a network of railways centred around a main line running from the Calder Valley route near Sowerby Bridge, through Halifax and approaching Leeds from the Bramley direction. Unfortunately, the WRUR never actually built its railway, as it became part of the merger of several railway companies in 1847 that formed the Lancashire and Yorkshire Railway Company. Initially, this new company had many other priorities that took precedence over the construction of the WRUR and the line was not proceeded with.

died during its construction. Notwithstanding this difficult gestation, the completed line opened on 9 July 1849. A temporary terminus was opened on Wellington Street, Leeds, until services were accommodated at Leeds Central and then at the Midland Railway's Wellington Street Station.

The final railway to approach Leeds during the period of the railway mania was the Great Northern Railway. As early as 1836, a railway to be called the Great Northern Railway was proposed. It would run from Whitechapel in East London via Cambridge and Lincoln to York. However, this was a stupendously ambitious project for such an early date and Parliament turned it down.

By 1844, there was only one trunk railway route from London to Scotland and that route utilized the London and Birmingham Railway, which was in alliance with the Grand Junction Railway. This in turn connected with the North Union Railway, giving access to Preston and Fleetwood. Hardy souls wishing to travel on to Scotland made use of a steamer service from Fleetwood to Ardrossan.

As already noted, this was the period of the railway mania, when a myriad of schemes, not all of them realistic, were promoted and anyone could get rich quickly if they were not caught with a failed scheme. George Hudson, the railway financier, was exceptionally skilled in promoting railways and having them built, and most particularly of neutralizing or destroying any opposition or competition to his lines.

Promoters wanted to build a railway from London to York with the ambition of an eastern trunk route to Scotland by way of a connection with the York and Darlington. After much negotiation with promoters of other lines that might connect with – or compete against – their line, a London and York Railway proposal was submitted to the 1845 session of Parliament. There were 224 railway bills in that session and the Board of Trade was instructed to set up a committee to assess groups of proposed lines. When the London and York Railway scheme came before the Parliamentary Committee, Hudson set up such a protracted series of objections that the project ran out of Parliamentary time. The London and York Railway scheme was re-submitted to the 1846 session of Parliament and, because some other schemes for railways to the north had by then fallen by the wayside, their supporters joined the London and York project. To reflect this greater support, the proposed company name was altered to the Great Northern Railway. George Hudson continued to use his dubious methods to frustrate the scheme but, on 26 June 1846, the Great Northern Railway Act was given the Royal Assent. Numerous branches earlier proposed had been deleted, including one from Doncaster to Leeds, but the main line was approved. Authorized capital was £5.6 million (about equivalent to £650m in 2020). The company had spent £590,355 (about £68m equivalent in 2020) on Parliamentary expenses. This was a clearly a massive undertaking with 'deep-pocketed' proprietors. The proposed route started at London (Pentonville) and passed through Huntingdon, Peterborough, Grantham, Retford, Doncaster and Selby to a junction with the Great North of England Railway just south of York station. Additionally, included in the Act, was a loop from Werrington Junction, north of Peterborough, via Spalding to Boston, Lincoln and Gainsborough, and then back on to the main line north of Bawtry.

1846 was a peak year for railway scheme authorizations, fuelled by the feverish hunt for quick riches in railway shares. For several reasons, not all connected with railways, there was a massive slump in the following year, and investment money, especially for railway projects already authorized, became almost impossible to get.

The Great Northern Railway directors had a dauntingly large railway network to build and they had to prioritize the parts of their authorized network that they would start to construct. In the second half of 1847, the directors, owing to the state of the money market, decided to abstain from letting the works from Doncaster to York. In spite of this hesitancy, at the end of July, a further small contract was let to Messrs Peto & Betts for the works from Doncaster, northwards to Askern, with the object of forming an 'end-on' junction there with the branch of the Lancashire and Yorkshire Railway, over

On 4 September 1965, ex-LMS Black Five 4-6-0, 44951, enters Leeds City Station with the 09:30 Manchester Exchange to Newcastle. The loco was based at nearby Mirfield and was a regular on these services. Note the crowds of enthusiasts collecting engine numbers. JOHN HUNT

LNER-designed Peppercorn A1 Pacific 4-6-2, 60145, *St Mungo,* awaits the 'right-away' from Leeds City Station in the summer of 1965, with a service that will take it back to its home depot of York (North).
JOHN HUNT

which the Great Northern had just obtained power to run its trains to Wakefield, Methley and Leeds.

The various stations in Leeds were 'crying out' for rationalization. The first to be opened was in 1834, when the Leeds and Selby Railway (a future constituent of the North Eastern Railway) opened its line to a terminus at Marsh Lane east of the city centre. In 1840, the North Midland Railway (a future constituent of the Midland Railway) constructed its line from Derby to a terminus at Hunslet Lane to the south. In 1846, the line was extended to a more central location at Wellington Street, known as Wellington Station. Also on Wellington Street from 1854 was Leeds Central Railway Station, jointly owned by the L&NWR, the North Eastern Railway (NER), the Great Northern, and the Lancashire and Yorkshire.

In 1869, New Station opened as a joint enterprise by the L&NWR and the NER. It connected the former Leeds and Selby Railway Line to the east with the L&NWR lines to the west. A mile-long connection was built, carried entirely on viaducts and bridges. New Station was built partially on a bridge over the River Aire, adjacent to Wellington Railway Station.

Traffic continued to increase but no attempt was made to rationalize the number of stations for nearly seventy years. In 1938, two stations (New and Wellington) were combined to form Leeds City Station, opening on 2 May that year. The third railway station, Leeds Central, was unaffected by the change. Part of Wellington Railway Station later became a parcels depot. The north concourse and the Queens Hotel were built at the same time.

On 14 March 1941, Leeds City Station was bombed by the German Luftwaffe and, although severely damaged, was later rebuilt. In 1967, further remodelling of the site took place and trains using Central Railway Station were diverted into the City Railway Station, which became the main railway station serving the city. Central Railway Station was closed and demolished.

At the time of this rebuilding, the railway station was served by 500 trains on a typical day, with 2.75 million passenger journeys a year. Wellington (or City North) became a parcels depot with the track layout extensively changed. The remaining Midland Line trains, which previously used this station, were diverted into the Leeds City Station, the former L&NWR/NER 'new' station, and called simply Leeds from this time.

By the 1990s, the railway station's capacity was being exceeded on a daily basis, and the 1967 design was deemed inadequate. Between 1999 and 2002, a major rebuilding project took place, branded as 'Leeds First'. The project saw the construction of additional approach tracks at the western end of the railway station, improving efficiency by separating trains travelling to or from different destinations and preventing them from having to cross each other's routes. The railway station was expanded from twelve to seventeen platforms, with the construction of new platforms on the south side, and reopening of the now disused parcels depot to passengers on the north side. Most of the track, points and signals were also replaced and the 1967 power box closed – control being handed over to the signalling centre at York. The most visible change to passengers, however, was the replacement of the 1967 metal canopy with a new glass roof, considerably increasing the amount of daylight on the platforms. A new footbridge and lifts were provided, replacing the previous underpass. Ancillary improvements included a new multi-storey car park and railway station entrance, refurbishing of the north concourse and expanded retail facilities.

As the 1840s progressed, we begin to see the amalgamations that produced the main railway companies before the 1922 grouping. We have already noted the birth of the Midland Railway in 1844 and the Great Northern Railway in 1846. A further step in the amalgamation of the smaller railway companies came in 1847, when the Manchester and Huddersfield Railway and Canal Company leased itself to the London and North Western Railway together with the connecting Leeds Dewsbury and Manchester Railway. In the same year, the Lancashire and Yorkshire Railway acquired the Leeds and Manchester Railway, which meant that just two major railway companies controlled the two competing routes between Manchester and Leeds.

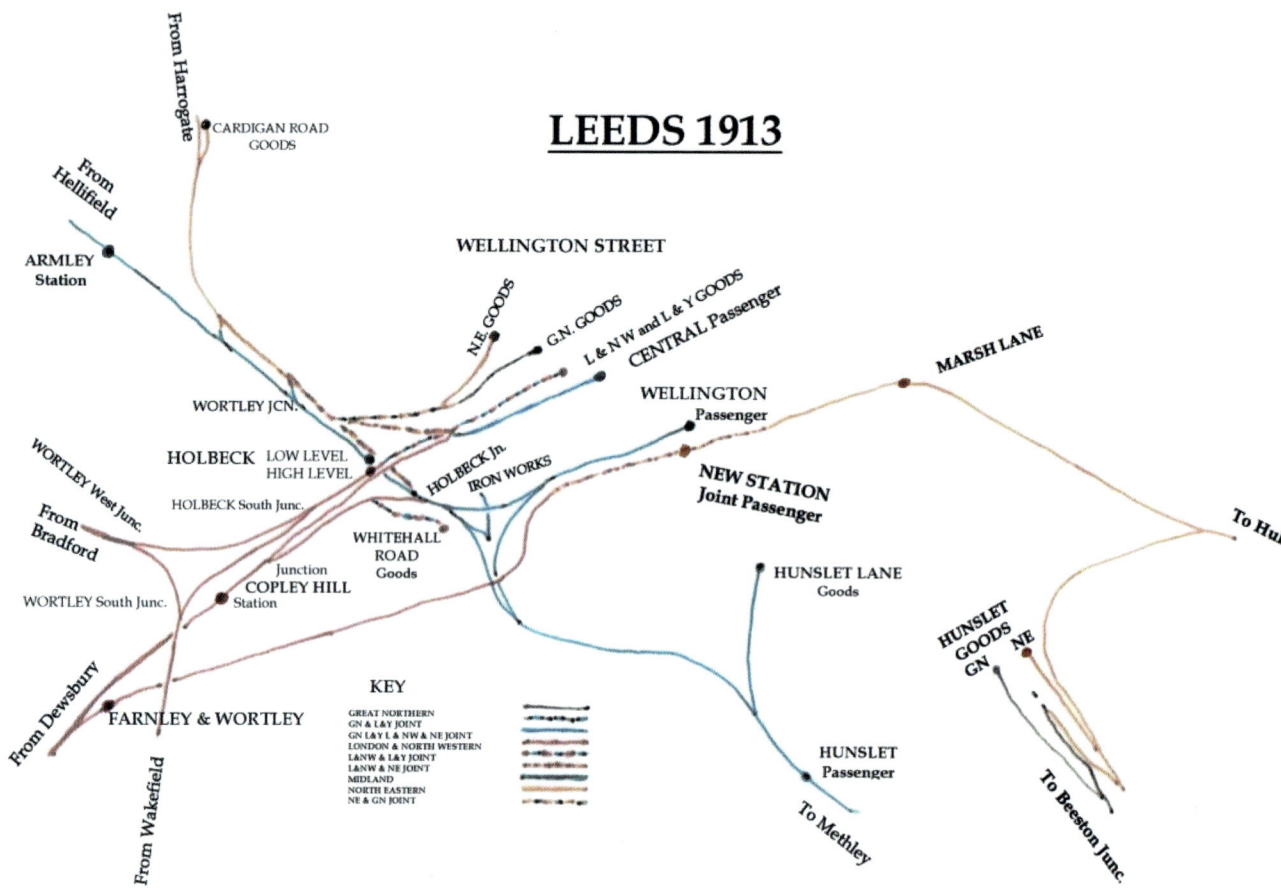

Leeds stations.

Seventy-five years later, the two companies would merge and become part of the London Midland and Scottish Railway (LMSR) at the 1923 grouping. By the end of the nineteenth century, traffic was so great that the L&NWR built a new line to duplicate the existing route through Batley, from Heaton Lodge Junction east of Huddersfield via Cleckheaton, regaining L&NWR metals at Farnley Junction, just south of Leeds. This became known as the 'Leeds New Line'.

The Leeds and Thirsk Railway, which, as we have seen, opened throughout on 9 July 1849, sought permission from Parliament to extend its line to Stockton. This was granted and received Royal Assent on 16 July 1846. The line was opened formally on 15 May 1852 and public traffic started on 2 June. The Leeds and Thirsk Railway received permission to change its name to the Leeds Northern Railway on 3 July 1851. In the following year, after the Leeds Northern Railway had reached Stockton and made an alliance with the West Hartlepool Harbour and Railway, a price war broke out with the York, Newcastle and Berwick Railway (YN&BR), the fare for 238 miles (383km) between Leeds and Newcastle dropping to two shillings. T. E. Harrison, who had become general manager and engineer of the YN&BR, looked at merger of that railway with Leeds Northern and York and North Midland as the answer. With a proposal that the shares of the three companies remain separate, replaced by Berwick Capital Stock, York Capital Stock and Leeds Capital Stock, and dividends paid from pooled revenue,

The twelve-road 'dead-end' shed at Farnley Junction dating from 1882 and seen here on Sunday 18 July 1965. With closure looming (which came in October 1966), there is a general air of neglect about the place. By then there were only twelve engines allocated, most of those were ex-LMS Black Fives with a handful of class 8s. JOHN HUNT

Ex-LMS Jubilee, Kolhapur, strides confidently past Wortley Junction on 26 August 1967 in the final weeks of its working life with BR. New in December 1934, it was named in May 1936. After nationalization in 1948, it was renumbered 45593 and was allocated to various sheds during the 1950s and 1960s, including Carlisle Upperby, Willesden and, in March 1965, to Leeds Holbeck, where it was kept in good condition to work railtours over the Settle and Carlisle line. In January 1968, it was bought for preservation and is currently based at Tyseley, Birmingham. JOHN HUNT the agreement of the three boards was reached in November 1852. However, the deal was rejected by the shareholders of the Leeds Northern, who felt that their 7 per cent share of revenue was too low; joint operation was agreed instead of a full merger and Harrison appointed as general manager. The benefits of this joint working allowed Harrison to raise the offer to the Leeds Northern shareholders and, by Royal Assent on 31 July 1854, the three companies merged and became the North Eastern Railway; with 703 route miles (1,131km) of line, it became the largest railway company in the country at the time.

By 1860, the network of railways serving Leeds had been established:

- The Great Northern Railway providing Leeds with a service from Central Station to London and to Bradford.
- The North Eastern Railway providing services from New Station to York, Harrogate, Newcastle and Hull.
- The London and North Western Railway from New Station, serving the Leeds to Manchester and Liverpool corridor via Huddersfield.
- The Lancashire and Yorkshire Railway from Central Station, also serving the Leeds to Manchester route but by the longer Calder Valley line.
- The Midland Railway providing more local services, from Wellington Station, to Shipley and thence dividing to serve Bradford and Skipton.

However, the opening of the Settle and Carlisle line in 1876 catapulted the Midland Railway Co. into the league of major railway passenger companies with the introduction of through services from London to Glasgow, passing through Leeds (Wellington). The Midland gained a reputation for luxurious carriages and the Great Northern (GN) was seriously affected by the competition that it now faced on the Leeds to London route. The GN hit back by introducing the first dining-car services in February 1880, which wooed back some of their erstwhile passengers. The

One of the sheds that did not survive beyond the steam age was Stourton. Originally built by the Midland Railway to service engines on its Leeds to Derby route, it was opened in 1875. Shown in this August 1965 picture is a Midland-designed Fowler 4F, 44570, new in August 1937, and looking to be in a very run-down state. Although a long-term resident at Stourton, having arrived there in 1951, it was withdrawn and sent for scrap just two months after the date of the picture. JOHN HUNT

Inside Stourton roundhouse on Sunday 18 July 1965, a day when many hard-pressed locos can be seen on shed together. No less than four heavy freight LMS-class 8Fs can be seen together with a former Midland Railway 4F and a BR Standard class 3. All had been withdrawn and sent for scrap by September 1967. JOHN HUNT

Stourton shed from the outside, as seen in July 1965. The main roundhouse is at the centre rear, with the offices and water tower to the right. The locomotives lined up in front of the tower are probably awaiting disposal. In the foreground is the ash pit, together with full and partially loaded wagons of ash for disposal. The locomotive in the centre is Royal Scot-class 4-6-0, 46115, Scots Guardsman, destined to enter preservation in the future. JOHN HUNT

Fast-forward forty-five years and Scots Guardsman *appears at platform 5 of York Station at the head of the West Coast Railway Company's Scarborough Spa Express on Thursday 12 August 2010.*

Midland responded in June by introducing vastly improved and accelerated services to London, but despite the GN temporarily cutting its timing to three and three-quarter hours, the Midland won the day and the GN had to discontinue three of its London services.

In the opposite direction, the Midland put on a through service to Edinburgh, but this did not catch on as it was found to be generally quicker by the North Eastern, even with a change at York.

Services to Sheffield were provided by the Midland but at various times other companies vied for the traffic. In July 1879, the Manchester, Sheffield and Lincolnshire Railway (later to become the Great Central Railway) put on a service from Central Station by means of running powers over the GN. It lapsed for nearly ten years between October 1893 and May 1903. The daily service ceased completely from March 1912. Not to be outdone, the GN ran a service on the same route but discontinued it after just a few months.

The original Holbeck shed was built by the Midland Railway and opened in May 1868. The main loco storage was by means of a roundhouse with a central turntable giving access to all roads. This view, from July 1965, shows three resident engines in the middle of the line with Jubilee-class India, 45574; 8F, 48104, and Ivatt-class 4, 43130. On the far left is a visitor from St Margaret's shed, Edinburgh, a Fairburn 2-6-4T, 42273. Finally, on the extreme right is a Black Five, 45445, from Lancaster Green Ayre. JOHN HUNT

The entrance to Holbeck loco shed did not set out to impress if arriving on foot! Seen not long before closure to steam in 1967. JOHN HUNT

Period cast-iron notices at the entrance to the Holbeck Roundhouse seen in 1965. JOHN HUNT

The NER also had a shed at Holbeck, close to the MR establishment, but the need for more and more locomotives to deal with the ever-expanding mineral traffic led to a new depot being built at Neville Hill, east of Leeds Station on the Leeds and Selby line in 1894. The site rapidly became one of the NER's bigger sheds still with an allocation of over eighty locomotives in the early 1950s. This view, from July 1965, shows Gresley V2, 2-6-2, 60810, preparing to come off shed. JOHN HUNT

Also seen inside Neville Hill shed, in July 1965, was this GER-designed L77 (LNER N7) 0-6-2T, 69621. Withdrawn in September 1962, the N7 had been privately purchased for preservation and was enjoying the 'hospitality' of Neville Hill shed whilst its future location was decided. Despite the initials on the tank sides, it was always a LNER/BR engine having been built at Stratford Works, East London in 1924. JOHN HUNT

To provide locomotives for these services required investment in locomotive servicing and storage facilities by all the companies involved. There was little sharing in the competitive atmosphere prevailing. Servicing facilities for current traction units are still provided on some of the sites today: the former NER Neville Hill and the Midland Railway (MR) Holbeck sites are two cases in point. In the days of steam traction, many more sites were active: Farnley Junction (L&NWR), Stourton (MR), Wortley Junction (GN), Copley Hill (L&NWR).

Today, Leeds Railway Station is a major and very busy transport hub. Maintained by Network Rail, it is used by London and North Eastern Railway (LNER), which provided high-speed trains to London, Harrogate and Bradford. CrossCountry trains provide services from Scotland to the Midlands, the South Coast and the West Country, with TransPennine Express operating between the North East, Manchester (and the Airport), Liverpool, Blackpool and Glasgow. Local services are provided by Northern to Harrogate, York, Doncaster, Hull, Sheffield, Huddersfield, Bradford, Skipton and all points in between. Leeds Station is the busiest station in the North of England, serving nearly 30 million passengers a year. It is also the third busiest British railway station outside London. With seventeen platforms, it is also the largest in terms of platforms numbers in England outside London, with eleven terminating and six through platforms.

CHAPTER 3

The Influence of York

A map of the Ridings of Yorkshire will show York sitting astride the confluence of the boundaries of all three Ridings. This strategic location was selected by the Romans in their quest for fortresses to keep the plundering natives (the Brigantes) under control, which was totally different from its later administrative role.

Roman York

Prior to the Roman occupation of Northern Britain, the land was controlled by the Brigantes, a loose federation of Celtic tribal groups. Their Queen, Cartimandua, favoured working with the Romans, unlike her estranged husband Venutius. The first-century historian, Tacitus, relates that when they separated, Venutius took up arms against the Queen and then against her Roman protectors. These skirmishes led to the Romans building fortifications on the frontier between their province and the Brigantes, including a fort near Rotherham. Further domestic disputes between Cartimandua and Venutius escalated the fighting in AD69 and sorely tried the neighbouring Romans' patience.

By AD71, the Romans had had enough. It was time for the invaders to impose their authority on the troublesome northerners and, in around AD71, the Roman Governor of Britain, Quintus Petilius Cerealis, set out with 5,000 troops from Lincoln (Lindum), crossed the Humber at Winteringham, landed at Brough (Petuaria) and marched inland. If anywhere exemplifies the Romans' skill at identifying the perfect site for a fortress, York (Eboracum) is it. When the Ninth Legion arrived, there wasn't much to see. No evidence has been found for a permanent native settlement in the heart of York prior to the Romans, so they would most likely have found before them little more than meadowland. Being the spot where the river Foss joins the river Ouse gives York an obvious strategic appeal. Men and supplies could be transported from the North Sea to the settlement via the Ouse. York also offered ease of land transport – it sits on a ridge that the Romans used as their main approach to the fort. This same route is still largely followed today by the main road, the A64.

The Romans chose to site their fortress not on the higher land, but down between the two rivers. What they lost in height they gained by the defensive advantage of having the rivers on both sides. In addition, it stood on a slightly raised plateau that would have been more prominent in Roman times when rivers were as much as three metres lower than they are today.

York had undoubted advantages for the task in hand. It was the ideal spot to launch attacks against

Brigantian resistance in the North York moors and the Pennine valleys, and became the stepping-off point for the Romans' military forays against Scotland.

The Romans remained until about AD400, when Anglo-Saxons took over the area and adapted the name to Old English, Eoforwíc or Eoforíc, which means 'wild-boar town' or 'rich in wild-boar'. The Vikings, who took over the area later, in turn adapted the name to Norse, Jórvík, meaning 'horse bay.'

Medieval York: Merchants, Trades, Prosperity and Decline

After the Anglian settlement of the North of England, Anglian York was first capital of Deira and later Northumbria. By the early seventh century, York was an important royal centre for the Northumbrian kings.

Following the Norman Conquest of 1066, York was substantially damaged, but in time became an important urban settlement as the administrative centre of the county of Yorkshire. For most of the Norman period, York, like the rest of Yorkshire, had been governed by the sheriff. He was based at York Castle but had responsibility for the whole county and wasn't accountable to the citizens. This all changed at the beginning of the thirteenth century.

As York's merchants grew richer, they resented the Sheriff of Yorkshire's dominance. Leading citizens banded together and became an influential voice in the city's affairs. It was King John who gave them the chance of self-government. Disastrous and expensive military campaigns left him sorely in need of funds, and one way to raise them was to allow a town's citizens to buy the right to rule themselves. The same pressures forced John, in 1215, to sign the Magna Carta, the charter giving some fundamental rights to the nation. York's own charter came three years earlier, in 1212, when King John allowed York's citizens, rather than the sheriff, to collect and pay the annual tax to the Crown, to hold their own courts and to appoint a mayor. From then on, until local government reorganization in 1974, York was a self-governing city under its own mayors. Hugh Selby, who exported wool and imported wine, became York's first known mayor in 1217. His family made the role their own: he was appointed a further five times, his son John seven times and his grandson Nicholas four times! The sheriff's remaining power was effectively stripped from him in 1256 by two charters from Henry III, which handed over control of the law and justice to the people of York.

However, not just anyone could trade in York in the Middle Ages – if you wanted to sell goods in the city, you had to be a freeman. You could buy the privilege, inherit it or work for it through an apprenticeship. It is the first record of the men – and, occasionally, women – who were merchants and had gained the freedom of the city. The freeman's register gives an insight into the most prominent trades, with the first one, produced in 1272, revealing the occupations of 452 freemen and shows that nearly 60 per cent were engaged in provisions and the leather trade. A further 29 per cent were engaged in metal, textile and building crafts with 10 per cent in commerce and shipping.

By the fifteenth century, the city was thriving and the freeman's register, alongside other documents, including taxation records and wills, gives a revealing picture of York's economy. The city's workers belonged to six broad groups:

- Woollen textile industry – almost a quarter of the male taxpayers in the town were involved in the cloth industry in one way or another.
- Leather industry – 10 per cent worked as skinners, tanners, saddlers or cordwainers making shoes. York had become the main centre for the production of high-quality leather goods in the country.
- Provisions – another 10 per cent worked in providing food and drink. As well as the bakers, butchers and fishmongers that you would find in any medieval town, there were also many grocers, spicers, salters and saucemakers in York, thanks to the number of visitors it attracted. The city's regional importance is also reflected in the many taverners and inn-keepers.
- Metal crafts – another near-tenth of freemen worked in the metal industry. Most were at a basic

level – smiths, cutlers, pin-makers and the like – but York also had an unusually high number of goldsmiths. People would turn to York for the latest in pewter tableware, for well-made cutlery and armour and to cast bells – the most demanding skill of all.
- Building work – includes the stone masons and carpenters, who made such a contribution to the look of the medieval town, and many more workers lost to obscurity.
- Specialized craftsmen – most notably the master glaziers who designed the windows in the minster and the many parish churches.

Those who didn't have the freedom of the city, or came from beyond York's boundaries, were called 'aliens' or foreigners. Overseas traders sometimes settled in York.

Whilst traditional crafts prospered, even more money was being made by the merchants who imported and exported, sending ships overseas via the port of Hull, from where smaller boats came upriver to York. Major local exports included grain and wool. The key overseas markets were the Low Countries, Germany, France and the Baltic. Wine was imported, first from France and then from further afield.

In around 1155, Henry II confirmed the city merchants' trading rights in England and Normandy with a charter, attested by Thomas Becket, which is the oldest document in the City of York Archives. Later, Richard I, 'the Lionheart', needing funds for a crusade, granted York valuable trading privileges in return for £133 – a handsome sum.

In 1203–04, York was ranked seventh in importance among ports of the south and east coast. Throughout the Middle Ages, docks and stores were maintained on the riverside. However, the tides worked against York: a boat could be stranded for a fortnight in the city if a tide was missed at certain times in the year. This detriment saw Hull grow in importance as the main Yorkshire port in the thirteenth century. Despite this, York retained its shipbuilding industry, having 69 shipwrights; more than anywhere else in the country in 1294.

York prospered during much of the later medieval era; the later years of the fourteenth and the earlier years of the fifteenth centuries were characterized by particular prosperity.

Towards the end of the Middle Ages, economic decline set in. The cloth industry, the mainstay of the city's economy in the fourteenth century, gradually moved to other parts of Yorkshire. York was expensive and highly regulated compared with smaller towns such as Halifax, Wakefield and Leeds. By the late fifteenth century, the industry had all but gone and had not been replaced. The population was falling, rents were low and many houses were derelict. To cap it all, York had backed the losing side in the War of the Roses. The city entered the Tudor age in its weakest state for centuries. Henry VIII succeeded his father to the throne in 1509 and during his reign, York would hit rock bottom. Unable to balance its books, it was bailed out by a central government that acknowledged that York could no longer pay the taxation levels set when it was a highly prosperous medieval metropolis.

York's Revival Prior to the Industrial Revolution

The abolition of the 'Council in the North' in 1641 did reduce York's status and its trade. During the English Civil War, the city was regarded as a Royalist stronghold and was besieged and eventually captured by Parliamentary forces under Lord Fairfax in 1644. After the war ended, York regained its pre-eminence in the North and, by 1660, was the third-largest city in England after London and Norwich. The city remained a religious and an administrative centre, both of which brought business. It was also developing as a social centre, thanks to the increasing fortunes of its wealthiest citizens. Both the aspiring gentry within the city walls and the newly leisured classes in the surrounding countryside had money to spend. London was too far away and York became the social capital of the north. Wigmakers, dressmakers and barbers set up shop in York. Booksellers, located near the printers in Minster Yard and Stonegate, sold the

About 10 miles south of York is Church Fenton, part of Hudson's original Y&NMR. The fine station seen here was opened by the NER in 1904, in conjunction with the quadrupling of the line to York. The train, hauled by now preserved LMS Black Five, 45428, was organized jointly by the Stephenson Locomotive Society and the Manchester Locomotive Society, and was to visit the NCB Ashington Colliery in Northumberland on 10 June 1967. JOHN HUNT

Passing through the Vale of York near Ulleskelf on the Y&NMR in July 2008, is preserved LMS Black Five 4-6-0, 45407. Complete with support coach, it is travelling from the Keighley and Worth Valley Railway's 40th Anniversary gala to the North York Moors Railway at Grosmont.

latest books. News and gossip was exchanged in the great inns, such as the George in Coney Street, or in the increasing number of coffee shops. In the best stores, Eastern silks and rugs, French wine and spices from the New World were sold.

Commerce was still strictly controlled, and non-freemen traders could be hit by heavy fines. The freedom of the city could be purchased, but it did not come cheap: in 1694 it was set at £20. However, it was still possible to gain the city freedom by apprenticeship or inheritance. Most York workers were employed in providing food and drink, clothing or buildings. Manufacturing was only a small part of the city economy. Other trades reflected York's growing prosperity, among them bookbinders, booksellers, stationers, pipe-makers, clockmakers, cabinet-makers and dancing masters. The markets and fairs remained important and were closely regulated by the corporation. Inns were booming and the corporation had only limited success acting against unlicensed alehouses. York had become a centre of commerce, leisure and social activity – a role that it quietly grew into during the eighteenth century. Significantly, the industrial age exploded elsewhere.

The population stayed steady at about 12,000 for the first sixty years of the eighteenth century, before climbing to about 17,000 in 1800. By contrast, Birmingham, Bristol, Leeds, Liverpool and Manchester all had populations of more than 50,000, and London was a city of 900,000 people by the end of the century.

The Industrial Revolution

The start of the Industrial Revolution saw new opportunities driven by inventions like the powered loom. Production of cloth moved from the front room to the factory and, as we have seen, large parts of Yorkshire and Lancashire began to grow rich on the textile industry. Mass industrialization bypassed York, perhaps because of the ironically named 'freedom regulations', which restricted trade. But York was far from a backwater. Still the seat of the archbishop, the city benefited from all the church officialdom, which came with this position. It remained Yorkshire's county town, and a regional administrative and legal centre. Its tradition as a military town continued with the building of cavalry barracks.

The city carved out a new role. It became the playground of the nobility and gentry, a city with fine assembly rooms for dancing and dining, a mansion house for mayoral banquets and a racecourse for sport. York in the eighteenth century benefited not from factories, but from a series of rather fine new buildings. York was fortunate to undergo a building boom at a time of great architectural style. As new materials were developed, red-brick buildings took the place of half-timbered houses and shops.

It was becoming easier for people to get about both by water and by road. The Foss and the Ouse had been used as a means of transport for centuries. The new canal technology enabled a dam to be built at Naburn Lock in 1757. This raised the level of the water and the navigability of York's River Ouse was no longer at the mercy of the tides. Parts of the Foss were also canalized to quicken its flow. The money for these works came from a toll on river cargoes, generally charged at sixpence a ton (0.9 tonne).

Another toll – the turnpike – brought great improvements to the roads. More than 150 miles (240km) of roads leading into York were maintained by turnpike trusts, thanks to the charge they levied on traffic. The level of payment depended on the size of the transport: on the busiest stretch of road, between Tadcaster and York, the charge was one shilling for a coach and six horses down to one penny for a horse and rider.

Due to these improvements in the nation's roads, journey times from York to London fell quickly. At the start of the eighteenth century it took four days to reach the capital; at the end, less than thirty-six hours. Every day in 1796, three daily coaches ran to London, two ran to Leeds and a Royal Mail coach went to Liverpool. London coaches departed from the Black Swan in Coney Street or the York Tavern in St Helen's Square. Services for the east coast and Hull left from the White Swan in Pavement. These new connections did allow York to begin to develop

Preserved LMS Coronation class Pacific 4-6-2, 6233, Duchess of Sutherland, sported this unusual black livery in 2010. Passing the site of Bolton Percy Station in a southerly direction on the Y&NMR line on 10 April 2010, it is working the return leg of an excursion from Leicester to Scarborough.

as a tourist destination, but they didn't bring the massive changes in industry and growth that many other cities were seeing at the time.

Trade in York Prior to the Industrial Revolution

The Industrial Revolution, initially, had far less impact on York than on other cities, which partly explains its charm today. At the beginning of the nineteenth century, York was the sixteenth-largest city in England; at the end, it was forty-first. In Yorkshire, Bradford, Halifax and Huddersfield outgrew the county's capital, which remained, at its heart, a market town. Although it functioned as an administrative centre, York had no clearly defined commercial role in the first half of the nineteenth century. Many trades were still restricted to freemen. It was a city of shopkeepers and innkeepers, chemists and domestic servants. Three glass works employed a few dozen people, but most manufacturing was on an even smaller scale. There were various family firms making everything from combs to musical instruments, farming tools to flax. The city still revolved around its markets and fairs. Wool was sold from Peasholme Green, an expanded cattle market opened outside Walmgate Bar in 1827, the fish market was held in St Sampson's Square and all manner of stallholders filled the new Parliament Street from 1836.

An unidentified BR class 37 Diesel loco makes its way over the intricate track work between Holgate Reception sidings and York South Yard in June 1976.

Nevertheless, York did grow, and more quickly than the likes of Norwich and Bath. For all but three decades during the century, the population of York increased by between 10 and 15 per cent. Fewer than 17,000 people lived there in 1801; more than 54,700 were York citizens a hundred years later.

The Coming of the Railways to York

It was the coming of the railways that brought the benefits of the Industrial Revolution to York. That it happened at all was not down to any great strategic guiding hand, but more to do with a desire to make money from investment. As we saw in Chapter 2, one man, George Hudson, is forever linked with the development of railways in York: by chance, Hudson met George Stephenson in Whitby and they became friends and business associates. Stephenson confided his long-held dream of a railway from London to Newcastle with a route leaving the London and Birmingham Railway near Rugby, passing through Derby and Leeds but omitting York. Hudson, alarmed at the proposed bypassing of his home town, pointed out that since 1833 there were already two railways proposed between Birmingham and Derby, which would link with the North Midland Railway from Derby to Leeds, and the York railway committee's proposed line from Leeds to York. From York, a line to Newcastle would probably garner wide investor support. The outcome of this conversation is not recorded but very soon after, another railway was being planned that would link York to Darlington, called the Great

In August 2009, there was an almost daily steam train to Scarborough from York. In this view, under the impressive curved train shed of platform 5, LMS Coronation Pacific 4-6-2, 6233, Duchess of Sutherland (in more conventional LMS maroon livery) pauses to collect passengers.

The original York Terminal Station was used by the LNER from about 1928 onwards as a railway museum. At the time, many railway companies were unable to provide storage space. The Great Western Railway (GWR), for this reason, destroyed the original broad-gauge locomotives, North Star and Lord of the Isles. The LNER took a more enlightened view and even preserved locomotives from other operators, such as City of Truro from the GWR. In this view of the original York Museum, we see GNR Stirling Single No 1 in the rather cramped display. The 4-2-2 was famed for its part in the 1895 'Race to the North'.

JOHN HUNT

North of England Railway (GNER). Its promoters hoped that it would be part of an East Coast route to Scotland and whilst initially favouring Leeds as their southernmost destination, they eventually chose York, although Hudson had little to do with this decision.

In 1835, the York railway committee became the York and North Midland Railway (Y&NMR) and at Hudson's suggestion the new line would join the North Midland at Normanton a few miles south-east of Leeds. The Y&NMR received its Act of Parliament on 21 June 1836 and, at its first official meeting, Hudson was elected chairman. Construction began in April 1837 and opened to a junction on the Leeds to Selby line on 29 May 1839 and to Normanton on 1 July 1840, meaning London was now linked by rail to York.

It has been claimed that the railways saved York from stagnation, but no one could have predicted the profound effect that this new form of transport would have on the city. In 1840, the first train ran direct from York to London. By the 1850s, there were thirteen trains a day between the two cities,

Inside York (North) engine shed in June 1965, showing one of the two turntables with storage roads radiating from them. In the picture can be seen two NER P3s (LNER J27s), one of which – 65894 – was later saved for preservation by the North Eastern Locomotive Preservation Group, a WD 2-8-0, two LNER Peppercorn 4-6-2 Pacifics and a LMS Ivatt-class 4MT. Except for the WD, all were York-based engines but all had been withdrawn by the end of September 1967. The site eventually became the National Railway Museum with both turntables featured. However, in a subsequent re-configuration, the second table was removed and sold to the North York Moors Railway, where it can be seen in operation at Pickering Station from time to time. JOHN HUNT carrying 341,000 passengers a year. In 1877, a new station, the largest in the country at the time, opened to accommodate them. By 1888, there were 294 trains arriving daily.

The impact of the railways on York was dramatic. The stage coaches declined, but much of the rest of the city was rejuvenated. The rail revolution allowed people and products to be transported to and from York faster than ever before. Entrepreneurs were given access to new markets. Tourism boomed: within two years of the first train steaming into York, excursions to the historic city were arriving from Manchester, Nottingham and London. Theatregoers came from miles around to see productions at the Theatre Royal, rebuilt four times in the nineteenth century. Two fine art and industrial exhibitions, in 1860 and 1879, at York Art Gallery, attracted a total of nearly 870,000 people, demonstrating the new mass mobility of the railway age. It also revolutionized communications. By the mid-1860s, York had two postal deliveries a day; a letter posted in London before noon was delivered in York the same evening.

The railways brought the city into the industrial age by introducing heavy industry for the first time. The repair and manufacture of engines and carriages became as important to the city as the railways themselves. In 1839, a small repair shop was opened on Queen Street. This expanded until, by 1849, it was repairing engines to the tune of £15,000 a year. The work on engines was carried on in York until about 1905. Of even greater significance though, was the carriage and wagon works, also at Queen Street, which could produce 100 wagons a week by 1864. In the 1880s, the North Eastern Railway decided to concentrate on carriage building in York. A new works was constructed in 1880–81 in Holgate. This rapidly expanded until, by 1910, it covered an area of 45 acres (18ha). In 1855, the 1,200-strong workforce was calculated to be earning £1,350 a week for the city's economy. By the end of the nineteenth century, York had around 5,500 railway employees, half of whom were employed in the carriage and wagon works, which remained active until 1996.

York Carriage and Wagon Works

Capacity for both the carriage and wagon building at the Queen Street Works was soon taken up. In 1867, the NER decided to move wagon building and repair to a new location, leaving Queen Street to specialize in carriage building. Even this move did not facilitate sufficient carriage-building capacity, so, by 1880, the NER took the decision to move carriage building to a new site at Holgate and let the first contracts for the construction of the new works in that year. The works were designed as an integrated carriage-building factory, with separate buildings for each process. The main buildings were of brick construction, with stone and coloured brick detailing. The internal construction was of cast-iron columns with wrought-iron beams. Carriage building started in 1884. By the late 1890s, capacity had again been reached, exacerbated by the increase in length of carriages, and, from 1897, contracts were let to expand the works, primarily to the west, plus a large lifting shop adjacent to the south of the main works building. Electric and gas shops were also added and additional stores, plus servicing and washing sheds, to the west. The expansion of buildings was mostly complete by 1900, excluding a wagon (rulley) shop built in 1904. (A rulley is a northern term for a flat wagon, usually horse drawn, and used for deliveries and extensively in agriculture in the nineteenth century.) A large wood-drying store allowed a ready supply of seasoned wood for carriage manufacture.

During the First World War, the York works produced material for the war effort, mostly logistics' equipment – existing carriage rolling stock was converted into ambulance trains and a complete train was produced for the Director General of Transportation.

In 1920, the carriage works had 13½ acres (5.5ha) of buildings on a site of 45 acres (18ha). The works built all the coaching stock of the NER, plus much of the East Coast Joint Stock and Great Northern and North Eastern Joint Stock, as well as undertaking most of the NER's carriage repairs. Overall, the carriage works employed 1,500 persons.

In the late 1970s British Rail Class 40, 40184, approaches Dringhouses Yard, York, with a train of tankers. JOHN HUNT

The NER was a major constituent of the LNER, formed by the grouping of 1923.

The LNER added traversers (*c*.1930s) at the west and east ends of the main works building on the south side and to accommodate the east traverser, the buildings were shortened.

During the Second World War, the carriage works produced parts for Horsa gliders. In 1944, part of the north building (the building shop), which had been manufacturing launches for the Royal Navy, was destroyed by an accidental fire. The building was rebuilt with a new roof featuring clerestory lighting. During the war, many of the workers were women, who worked shifts up to sixty-nine hours a week.

After the war, the works, along with the rest of the railway system, were nationalized and employed around 5,000 people. During the 1950s, there were still over 3,000 staff employed and early diesel multiple units were maintained on the site. Some early electric multiple unit trains were built at York, including the BR Class 305/1. In 1970, the rolling stock workshops division of British Rail (excluding repair works) became British Rail Engineering Limited (BREL). From the 1970s to 1989, the works manufactured much of British Rail's electric multiple unit passenger stock. The works continued producing vehicles for British Rail after privatization.

BREL was privatized in 1987, as BREL (1988) Ltd, and was acquired, in 1989, by a consortium including management, Trafalgar House and Asea Brown Boveri (ABB). In 1992, ABB acquired the company outright, including the York works. Procurement contracts on British Rail began being put to public tender in the 1980s. The fate of the works was linked primarily to the number of orders for Network South-East for electric passenger stock – failure to win the contract for electric multiple units for the Heathrow Express service (awarded to Siemens/CAF) resulted in the loss of 289 jobs. However, despite this loss, the works continued to win orders in the short term, but, by 1995, the 'writing was on the wall' when ABB announced that the factory would close due to lack of orders; the cause was widely recognized as being due to a gap in train orders caused by uncertainties following the privatization of British Rail. The carriage works closed in 1996 with 750 redundancies.

The Acquisitive York and North Midland Railway

Returning to York in the early Victorian period, it becomes clear that the York and North Midland Railway (Y&NMR), under Hudson's chairmanship, was an acquisitive railway always on the lookout for ways to expand. On 27 July 1840, it opened a curve connecting to the North Midland Railway at Methley Junction, near Castleford, facilitating the Y&NMR a direct access to Leeds, in competition with the ailing Leeds and Selby Railway (L&SR). From 9 November, Hudson leased the L&SR line for £17,000 per year; from then all traffic between Leeds and Selby was diverted via Methley and over the North Midland Railway to its Wellington Station. However, the management of the adjacent Hull and Selby Railway (H&SR) refused any offers from Hudson to lease or operate over their line, frustrating his desire to have a direct line from York to Hull. By 1844, the directors of the H&SR formed an alliance with the Manchester and Leeds Railway, which was planning a route to Selby, and amalgamation of the two companies was proposed early in 1845. However, the shareholders had different ideas and at two meetings over-ruled the directors, accepting instead a lease from Hudson at 10 per cent of the original capital, with an option to purchase. The H&SR became part of the Y&NMR from 1 July 1845.

The rapid expansion of the Y&NMR continued as the railway mania intensified, receiving permission, in 1844, to build a line from York to Scarborough with a branch from Rillington to Pickering, and to take over the Whitby and Pickering Railway. The 42-mile line (68km) and 6½-mile branch (10.5km) were built in less than a year and opened on 7 July 1845.

At the same time, further authority was granted by Parliament for a line to Harrogate, which was opened to Spofforth on 10 August 1847. After completing the 825yd-long (754m) Prospect Hill tunnel and 1,873ft-long (571m) Crimple Viaduct on 20 July 1848, services started to the centrally sited Brunswick Station.

Both the Y&NMR and H&SR had permission for lines to Bridlington: the Y&NMR from Seamer, on the York to Scarborough Line, and the H&SR from Hull. Both lines were built and opened on 6 October 1846. Parliamentary approval for two lines to Market Weighton was granted to the Y&NMR on 18

In August 2010, Northern Rail Class 142 DMU, 142027, waits in platform 8 at York Station ready to work the 14:11 service to Leeds via Harrogate.

June 1846. A twin-track York to Beverley line was opened to Market Weighton on 4 October 1847, and a single line from Selby to Market Weighton opened on 1 August 1848.

By the mid-1840s, as the railway mania subsided and investors started to take stock of promises made, it was becoming clear that some of Hudson's practices were illegal. By this time, apart from the Y&NMR, Hudson was also chairman of the Midland Railway, the Newcastle and Berwick and the Newcastle and Darlington Junction Railways. In 1845, to better promote the bills submitted by the railway companies he controlled, Hudson successfully stood as a Conservative Member of Parliament for Sunderland.

By 1848, the Great Northern Railway (GNR) had a route from London to Askern and the Y&NMR had authority for a branch from Burton Salmon to Knottingley, about 9 miles (14km) to the north. Hudson and Edmund Dennison, the chairman of the GNR, met at the end of 1848 and agreed terms for the GNR to access York via Knottingley, the GNR dropping plans for its own line to York via Selby. As this plan diverted traffic between York and London away from the London and North Western and Midland Railways, these two railways formed an alliance, attempting to divert whatever traffic they could via Leeds and handing it over to the York, Newcastle and Berwick Railway (YN&BR) at Thirsk.

At the end of 1848, the dividend paid by the Y&NMR dropped from 10 per cent to 6 per cent, and at a subsequent half-yearly shareholders meeting, the very high cost of certain GNER shares bought during the merger was questioned. After Hudson admitted the company had purchased them from him, an investigating committee was set up and Hudson resigned as chairman in May 1849. The committee reported on many irregularities in the accounts, such as inflating traffic figures and finding capital items that had been charged to the revenue account, thus paying dividends out of capital. No dividend was paid for the first half year of 1849, and Hudson had to pay out £212,000 to settle claims over share transactions.

The building of new branches was severely restricted in the years following Hudson's departure. Work was halted on a direct line between York and Leeds, although a stone viaduct had been built across the River Wharfe at Tadcaster, and an extension of the line from York to Market Weighton on to Beverley was suspended. However, the independent East and West Yorkshire Junction Railway had been authorized on 16 July 1846 to build a railway from the main line just outside York to Knaresborough. When it opened to a temporary station at Hay Park Lane on 30 October 1848, the line was worked by the YN&BR but, after 1849, this was switched to E. B. Wilson and Co, who were paid per mile plus a percentage of revenue. The railway was taken over by the Y&NMR on 1 July 1851.

The Y&NMR struggled to recover from the George Hudson scandal. In 1854, Parliamentary approval was granted for a merger with the York, Newcastle & Berwick Railway, the Leeds Northern Railway and the Malton and Driffield Railway to become the North Eastern Railway Company. York was chosen as the headquarters of the company, which on formation had a near monopoly on railways in the north-east and, importantly, controlled the middle section of the East Coast route to Scotland linking the Great Northern Railway near Doncaster with the North British Railway at Berwick-upon-Tweed.

York has had only three railway stations since the first train set off for Leeds in 1839. This first station was a temporary wooden building on Queen Street outside the walls of the city, opened in 1839 by the Y&NMR. It was succeeded in 1841, inside the walls, by what is now the York Old Station. Even George Hudson could not have foreseen how rapidly his railways would prosper. However, if he had he would have seen the folly of a terminal station serving a through route between London and Scotland. In due course, the irksome requirement that through trains between London, Newcastle and Scotland needed to reverse out of the York Old Station to continue their journey necessitated the construction of a new through station but outside the city walls. This (present) York Station was opened on 25 June 1877, replacing the original terminus of 1841, which was retained as the North Eastern Railway Head Office.

Platform 5 at York Station remains the principal departure point for important trains to Newcastle and Scotland. East Coast Class 91, 91128, draws in to the platform with the delayed Flying Scotsman 10:00 King's Cross to Edinburgh at 12:31 on Thursday 12 August 2010 (due 11:53).

In 1976, the author was privileged to be shown inside the main York Station power signal box, opened in 1951, which had replaced seven mechanical boxes. Inside, it had a hushed cathedral-like atmosphere, with subdued lighting that allowed the illuminated track display to dominate. As with all railway technology, things had moved on and, by 1989, the power box was replaced by the IECC (integrated electronic control centre), which in turn was replaced, in December 2018, by the York ROC (rail operating centre). The view inside the York power box shows the track display screens and the operator's console. This 1951 box was, at the time, one of the largest route-relay interlockings in the world, with its relay room 46m long by 10m wide, containing nearly 3,000 relays.

The post-Second World War layout of the station saw a multiplicity of tracks, including, as seen here, the middle through roads between platforms 3 and 5 for the use of passenger trains not stopping at the station and goods trains. Peppercorn-class K1 2-6-0, 62010, locally based at York North shed, emerges from the station on the up through line on 17 February 1964 with such a train.
JOHN HUNT

THE INFLUENCE OF YORK

ABOVE: *Sporting the then current operator's new livery, an East Coast HST set, headed by power car 43251, arrives at York Station platform 5 with the delayed* Northern Lights *10:30 King's Cross to Aberdeen on Thursday 12 August 2010 at 12:44 (due 12:25).*

LEFT: *LNER Peppercorn A1 Pacific 4-6-2, 60140,* Balmoral, *at the south end of York Station platform 5.* Balmoral *was a long-term resident at York North Shed, having been transferred there in June 1950. At the time of this picture, on 17 February 1964, the loco had less than a year left in service before withdrawal came in January 1965.* JOHN HUNT

RIGHT: *The roundhouse at York North Motive Power Depot (MPD) in 1965.*
JOHN HUNT

BELOW: *First Scotrail-liveried DBS Class 90, 90021, makes a speedy passage through York Station's platform 5 with the UK Railtours 'The Edinburgh Tattoo' charter on Thursday 12 August 2010.*

The design was conceived by Thomas Elliot Harrison, the NER engineer in chief, in collaboration with the company's architect, Thomas Prosser. Harrison devised the basic layout of the station and no doubt specified the trainshed roof form, leaving Prosser and his department to work out the details and prepare all the drawings. The resulting trainshed is one of the great iron 'cathedrals' of the railway age. Harrison did not favour enormous spans, such as the 245ft (77.5m) of St Pancras that

THE INFLUENCE OF YORK

BR Class 47, 47420, leaves York with a London-bound train in May 1981. Standing at platform 12 is the National Railway Museum's ex-LMS 46229, Duchess of Hamilton (clearly the reason for all the crowds of onlookers!) with an excursion train. Note the fine lines of the station roof. JOHN HUNT

In the 'diesel' era of 1970 to 1989 the BR Class 40s (or English Electric Type 4s) became popular with enthusiasts. To celebrate twenty-five years in service, a rail tour appropriately entitled 'The Silver Jubilee', was operated by BR using 40084 and 40086, seen here passing Dringhouses in the outskirts of York on 5 March 1983. The route was circuitous, passing through Leeds, Wakefield, Huddersfield and Stockport, and down the West Coast Main Line to London Euston. JOHN HUNT

The date is now August 2010 and the simplification of the 1988 track layout can be seen clearly, as can the impressive curved station roof. The train arriving at platform 5 is the daily excursion to Scarborough hauled by the National Railway Museum's Britannia-class locomotive 70013, Oliver Cromwell.

With the daily steam train to Scarborough, LMS Black Five 4-6-0, 45231, Sherwood Forester, strides out of York Station's platform 5 and crosses over to the Scarborough line on 28 August 2008.

With steam to spare, LMS Royal Scot-class, 46115, Scots Guardsman, eases the WCRC Scarborough Spa Express into platform 5 of York Station on Thursday 12 August 2010.

LMS 4-6-2 Pacific No 6233, *Duchess of Sutherland, heads north on the down slow line just past Skelton Junction, York, with the delayed Silver Jubilee excursion from London to Newcastle at 14:35 on Thursday 30 September 2010. The* Duchess *had taken over the train from LNER A4 Pacific 4-6-2, 60019,* Bittern, *at York and at this point the train was running about one-and-a-half hours late.*

A final image from York – 1988 was the fiftieth anniversary of LNER 4468, Mallard, *achieving the world speed record for steam traction. To mark this occasion, the National Railway Museum overhauled the loco and ran several excursions. One such excursion is seen here, on 16 July 1988, as the celebrity loco heads south under Holgate Road bridge.*
JOHN HUNT

opened almost a decade earlier. Instead, the York roof was subtly modulated, with a main span of 81ft (25m) and flanking ones of 55ft (16.5m), together with a further 45ft-span (13.5m) over the bay platforms on the entrance side. The outcome is a building that, although very large, does not upstage the city walls on their rampart opposite the station entrance. As constructed, it had thirteen platforms and was, at that time, the largest in the world. In 1909, new platforms were added and, in 1938, the current footbridge was built. The building was heavily bombed during the Second World War. On one occasion, on 29 April 1942, 800 passengers had to be evacuated from a King's Cross–Edinburgh train that arrived during a bombing raid. The station was extensively repaired in 1947 and designated as a Grade II* listed building in 1968.

The track layout through and around the station was remodelled again in 1988 as part of the re-signalling scheme that was carried out prior to the electrification of the East Coast Main Line (ECML) shortly afterwards. This was brought about by the changing nature of travellers to and from the station. In Victorian times, many services started from, or terminated at, the station. This changed with greater availability of personal transport in the mid-twentieth century and resulted in several bay platforms (mainly on the eastern side) being taken out of service and the track to them removed. In 2006–07, to improve facilities for bus, taxi and car users, as well as pedestrians and cyclists, the approaches to the station were reorganized. The former York north motive power depot and goods station became the National Railway Museum in 1975.

CONFECTIONERY IN YORK

The other major industry that became established in York was the manufacture of confectionery. The Western world discovered the cacao bean in the sixteenth century, but it wasn't until the Industrial Revolution that the complex process of turning the beans into cocoa and chocolate was mastered.

The confectionery and cocoa-processing industries were a key part of York's economy in the nineteenth century. Joseph Terry was established in 1838: first in confectionery, then in candied peel, and Thomas Craven produced sugar confectionery in York. One of the thirty-one tea dealers in the city, Samual Tuke, had begun to trade in coffee, and then he expanded into tea with the collapse of the East India Company's monopoly. Henry Isaac Rowntree acquired Tuke's business in 1862, his elder brother Joseph joining him in 1869. An added dimension to cocoa came in 1881 with the manufacture of gums and pastilles, a hitherto French speciality. At the beginning, the staple Rowntree's product was 'Rock Cocoa', later developed into the more palatable 'Elect Cocoa', first marketed in 1887. It was a quality product that was marketed as 'more than a drink, a food', and it challenged the idea that beer was essential to manual workers because it gave him sustenance as well as refreshment: Quaker cocoa was a temperance drink.

These cocoa manufacturers were the second-biggest employer in York, second only to the railways, and they could employ many women, thus making an impact on patterns of employment in York that were different from elsewhere.

First the rivers then the railways brought raw ingredients like cocoa, sugar and fruit rinds, into the city, and allowed the finished product to be sold far beyond York.

By this time, workers had a little disposable income and could treat themselves to the bars, pastilles and assortments created in the factories. The wealth generated by the new industries helped to create a class of citizens who were hungry for the finer things in life – including education and culture.

CHAPTER 4

The Rise and Rise of Doncaster

Early Doncaster

Doncaster grew up at the site of a Roman fort, believed to be called Danum, constructed in the first century at a crossing of the River Don, which provided an alternative direct land route between Lincoln (Lindum) and York (Ebor). The main route between Lincoln and York was Ermine Street, which required units to cross the River Humber in boats. Militarily, this was potentially hazardous and was difficult to defend from the Brigantian raiders. As a result, the Romans considered Doncaster to be an important and safe staging post.

Doncaster became an Anglo-Saxon Burgh, during which period it received its present name: 'Don-' from the Old English 'donne' meaning Roman settlement and 'caster' ('ceaster') from an Old English adaptation of the Latin 'castre' (military camp; fort and river).

As the thirteenth century approached, Doncaster matured into a busy town; in 1194, King Richard I granted it national recognition with a town charter. Over the next 400 years, Doncaster faced many disastrous events, starting with a fire in 1204, from which it only slowly recovered. Buildings were mostly built of wood, with open fireplaces used for cooking and heating, so the risk of fire was a constant hazard. By 1334, Doncaster was the wealthiest town in southern Yorkshire and the sixth most important town in Yorkshire, even boasting its own banker.

However, in the mid-fourteenth century, the entire country was swept by the Black Death (bubonic plague) and the population of Doncaster was reduced to less than 1,500. Several further outbreaks occurred in the late sixteenth and early seventeenth centuries, and each time the disease struck down significant numbers of the town's population. Despite this, the town continued to expand in the sixteenth and seventeenth centuries.

During the campaign of the First English Civil War, Charles I marched by way of Bridgnorth, Lichfield and Ashbourne to Doncaster, where, on 18 August 1645, he was met by great numbers of Yorkshire gentlemen who had rallied to his cause. On 2 May 1664, Doncaster was rewarded with the title of 'Free Borough' by way of the king (Charles I's son, King Charles II) expressing his gratitude for Doncaster's allegiance.

Doncaster as a Communication Hub

Doncaster has traditionally been a prosperous area and the borough was known for its rich landowners with vast estates and huge stately homes, such as Brodsworth Hall, Cantley Hall, Cusworth Hall, Hickleton Hall, Nether Hall and Wheatley Hall. This wealth is evidenced in the luxurious and historic, gilded eighteenth-century Mansion House on High Street. This land ownership developed over what is an ancient market place and large buildings were erected in the nineteenth century, including the Market Hall and the Corn Exchange. Perhaps the most striking building is St George's Minster, constructed in the nineteenth century and promoted from a parish church in 2004.

By the early nineteenth century, Doncaster was already a communications centre, due to its strategic geographical importance, sitting astride the Great North Road; this was the primary route for all traffic from London to Edinburgh.

Unlike other parts of the West Riding, the railways of the area were not particularly constrained by physical features. Scenically, the Pennine slopes merge into the southern end of the Vale of York, where the undulating foothills quickly give way to a vast area of largely flat arable land. As already noted, from medieval times the town's economy was dominated by the Great North Road. By the early nineteenth century, Doncaster had become famous for horse racing and had been noted as 'one of the most clean, airy and elegant towns in Britain'. For these reasons, and unlike other towns in the West Riding, Doncaster did nothing to encourage the coming of railways, this attitude being typified by its rejection of the 1830 Sheffield and Goole Railway as 'wholly unnecessary and uncalled for'. For this reason, there were no lines of any significance in the area until 1848.

That the town was to become a major railway centre was by no means certain in the 1840s. From the beginning of that decade, the route from London to York (and eventually Newcastle and Edinburgh) had become established using the London and Birmingham, the Midland Counties, the North Midland and the York and North Midland Railways. In 1844, the Midland Counties and the North Midland Railways (along with others) merged to become the Midland Railway. As chairman of the Midland and the York and North Midland Railways, George Hudson was not well disposed toward proposals from a new company, the Great Northern, for an entirely new trunk route to the north

THE YORKSHIRE COALFIELD

The South Yorkshire Coalfield stretches across most of the West Riding from Halifax in the north-west, Leeds in the north-east, Huddersfield and Sheffield in the west and Doncaster in the east. It is part of a larger Nottingham, Derbyshire and Yorkshire Coalfield, and the coal-bearing rock strata (coal measures) outcrop in the foothills of the Pennines, which slope from west to east. Because of its relative ease of mining, this area is known as the exposed coalfield. The coal measures are carboniferous rocks formed between 300 and 350 million years ago, but around Doncaster they are overlaid by limestone and, because of the difficulty in getting access to these deeper, buried measures, this area became known as the concealed coalfield.

There is evidence to suggest that coal-mining was taking place when the Romans colonized Britain. Certainly, there is evidence of such activity in the fourteenth century around Barnsley, Rotherham and Sheffield. These mines were shallow shafts or adits exploiting the coal measures where they outcropped. The coal would have been used locally as a heating fuel. Unlike mining in Northumberland and County Durham, which expanded rapidly at this time, the small-scale development in Yorkshire persisted until the mid-eighteenth century due to a lack of water transport.

However, in 1740, the River Don Navigation was canalized as far as Tinsley near Sheffield. This allowed the collieries near Rotherham to export their coal east to the English coast and beyond, and west to Sheffield. By 1769, 300,000 tons (272,155 tonnes) of coal were exported from the southern area of the coalfield. The Derbyshire coal owners noted this trade and commissioned a new waterway, the Chesterfield Canal, which ran to the River Trent at Gainsborough and was opened in 1777. Much like the railway age that was to follow, the canal age was very competitive and the South Yorkshire owners soon turned their attention to improving their waterway access to the sea. Sanction was gained for a canal from Wakefield, south through Barnsley to the River Don at Swinton, east of Rotherham. The Dearne and Dove Canal, as it became known, started construction in 1793 and was completed in 1796.

by way of Peterborough, Grantham, Doncaster and York, carefully avoiding the lines of the companies in which he had a financial interest. Had Hudson maintained his power base, then things might have been very different.

Whilst the demand for passenger services drove many of the proposals, the 'canny' Yorkshiremen knew that there was another traffic waiting in the wings – coal. Traditionally moved by water to the ports for trans-shipment to coasters for the sea journey to London and the southern counties, promoters of railways from Yorkshire to the south had their eyes firmly fixed on the major income stream to be had from winning contracts to transport this ever more popular mineral.

The Coming of the Great Northern Railway

Hudson's Midland Railway had already established a route to London via Derby from the early 1840s and quickly established a flow of traffic to the south in competition with the waterway companies. This proved to be very lucrative for the company and other potential railway undertakings urgently set about looking for routes to access this valuable traffic.

Despite Hudson's objections, the Great Northern Railway Act was passed in 1846, allowing the construction of a main line connecting London to York, via Peterborough and Doncaster, and then connecting with the Great North of England Railway just south of York Station.

Also with a part to play in the railways of Doncaster was the Manchester, Sheffield and Lincolnshire Railway (MS&LR). On 16 July 1849, the section of its main line from Woodhouse Junction, on the Sheffield–Beighton Junction section, to Gainsborough, was formally opened. This line crossed the proposed route of the Great Northern Railway (GNR) at Retford and made a junction with it at Gainsborough. By means of a reversal, GNR trains could use the MS&LR Gainsborough station.

The direct line between Peterborough and Doncaster was known as the Towns Line. The first part of it was opened between the MS&LR stations at Retford and Doncaster on 4 September 1849. By this means, the GNR could start a service between London and Leeds using running powers and agreements over other lines in a roundabout routing northward from Retford. George Hudson tried to repudiate his earlier undertaking to permit this, but by this time his financial misdemeanours had come to light and he had resigned from the Midland Railway and several other boards. The train service started on 1 October 1849.

Slightly earlier, the Wakefield, Pontefract and Goole Railway (WP&GR) had constructed a branch from its main line near Knottingley to Askern on the GNR just north of Doncaster. The Manchester and Leeds Railway saw benefit in working closely with the GNR and, as it was about to take over the WP&GR, entered into negotiations with the GNR to gain access to Doncaster from the north-east. For its part, the GNR was keen to use the WP&GR to gain access to Wakefield, Methley and on to Leeds. The formal agreement came in to force on 1 May 1847.

These were difficult times for George Hudson; he was astute enough to see that, unless he did something about it, the York and North Midland would not continue as the main conduit into York from the south with consequent, very significant loss of revenue to the new competitor, the GNR. To mitigate this risk, his first move was, in 1847, to promote a short, three-mile long branch, from the Y&NMR at Burton Salmon to the WP&GR at Knottingley. Its purpose purported to be mineral extraction and to give the local residents better access to Leeds and Hull. What Hudson was keeping quiet about was its momentous importance if it was to become a vital connection in a new East Coast route. Secret negotiations with the GNR followed with the aim of giving it access to the Y&NMR at Burton Salmon to reach York, in return for allowing Y&NMR trains to run south from Knottingley into Doncaster. For the GNR this was tempting. The long battle to get the bill through Parliament had left the company short of cash; capital was proving difficult to raise and so not having to fund the Doncaster–York section was attractive. The company was reported to have concerns about loss of independence but, in the end, the 'pros' outweighed the 'cons' and an agreement, coming in to force on 29 November 1850, was reached. Edmund Denison, the first chairman of the GNR was, subsequently, heard to lament that their new trunk railway, instead of reaching York, had ended up in a ploughed field four miles north of Doncaster!

Although the GNR seemed to be dominating railway developments in and around Doncaster, it was not the only player. In the 1846/7 session of Parliament, the South Yorkshire, Doncaster and Goole Railway Company (SYD&GR) was established on 22 July by an Act enabling it to acquire the permitted lines, south of Barnsley of the Sheffield, Rotherham, Barnsley, Wakefield, Huddersfield and Goole Railway (SRBWH&GR), make new lines and acquire the River Dun Navigation and the Dearne and Dove canals. The company's permitted lines were a main line from Doncaster to a junction with the Midland Railway at Swinton. The authorized share capital of the company was £750,000 in £20 shares.

Formal amalgamation with the Dun and Dearne canals took place on 12 April 1850. After amalgamation, the company became the South Yorkshire Railway and River Dun Company, but when referring to its railway activities, it was usually known as the South Yorkshire Railway (SYR).

Work on the Swinton to Doncaster main line was under way by October 1847; the first, ceremonial sod being cut in 'Warmsworth Field', the site of the present-day cutting. Work got behind schedule, but the line was ready for a trial run to take place on 29 October 1849, when a special train left Cherry Tree Lane Station, Doncaster. The station was located on the north-western side of the triangular junction with the GNR at Doncaster. The train, made up of two first-class carriages loaned by the Midland Railway and a GNR open wagon fitted with seats, was propelled by a four-coupled tank locomotive that had recently been used for ballasting the line. The Board of Trade inspector, Captain George Wynne, inspected the Doncaster–Swinton section of the line on 31 October 1849 and reported it as safe for use, also noting some deviations from the permitted line.

The date of opening was set for Saturday, 3 November, but unforeseen delays resulted in a week's postponement and the Swinton to Doncaster line was finally opened on 16 November 1849. The passenger service, to run from Sheffield, was to be operated by the Midland Railway and was timed to connect with their trains from the North, Derby, Birmingham, Gloucester, Bristol and London. At the opening, the only intermediate station on the SYR was Conisbrough, although further stations were added from 1 February 1850, to serve the villages of Mexborough and Sprotborough. The Midland Company worked the line with its engines and carriages in exchange for one-quarter of the receipts.

In the Parliamentary session of 1851, the South Yorkshire Railway and River Dun Company (SYR&RDCo.) applied for permission to lease, sell or amalgamate itself with the GNR and the SYR, and the River Dun Company's Transfer Act was passed in 1852. However, the amalgamation was not carried through and the process was abandoned by both companies.

In the mid-1850s, the SYR created a railway line from Doncaster to Thorne on the banks of the canals between the two towns. Surprisingly, the line was built without Parliamentary sanction for its construction, although the SYR owned all the land. The single-track line was 10 miles 44 chains (17km) long and ran along the southern bank of the River Don 'Flood Drain', starting from Marsh Lane Junction just north of Doncaster. After Long Sandall, it followed the north bank of the River Don Navigation, past Kirk Sandall, Barnby upon Don, Sand Bramwith to Stainforth, and thence along, or close to, the north bank of the Stainforth and Keadby Canal to Thorne. The line terminated at Thorne Waterside Railway Station (which was then the only station on the line), sometimes referred to as Thorne Lock because of its location. This was the first railway station to be opened in Thorne, with goods traffic carried from 11 December 1855. The line was passed as safe for passengers by the government inspector in June 1856, provided only one engine was in steam at any one time on the line and subject to a maximum speed of 12mph (19km/h) as curves were as tight as 8 chains (530ft/160m) radius; road crossings at Bramwith, Barnby Dun and Stainforth were also required to be manned. Passenger-carrying commenced on 7 July 1856. The station was adjacent to the Stainforth to Keadby Canal, convenient for trans-shipping goods traffic for forwarding on.

Passenger services lasted for around three years before being transferred to a new station, officially called Thorne but usually referred to as Thorne (Old) Railway Station. It was situated near the town centre on the first stage of the canal-side line to Keadby, which was opened in September 1859. The new line left the original SYR just before arriving at Thorne Waterside, taking a right-handed junction toward the town centre. When the line opened, this station was the terminus of the line. The canal-side line fell out of use after new 'straightened' lines were opened in 1864, with a new station, Thorne South, about a third of a mile to the south. Another station, Thorne North, to the north of the town centre, opened with the line to Hull in 1869.

Despite the failure of the proposed merger with the GNR in 1852, the company clearly saw its future as part of a larger undertaking. Relationships with the MS&LR were cordial and the company had allowed the use of Sheffield Victoria Station by the SYR. Discussions about closer working began in 1860 and, in 1861, the MS&LR began a lease of the SYR. Parliamentary approval was sought and on 23 June 1864 the South Yorkshire Railway and River Dun Transfer Act enabled the MS&LR to take over the SYR for 999 years. As part of the arrangement, the MS&LR was to pay the dividends and interests relating to SYR stock, and to give half of the net profits of the line to the South Yorkshire Company, with working expenses taken to be 38 per cent of gross profits for accounting purposes. Ten years later, the SYR was dissolved by the South Yorkshire Railway and River Dun Company's Vesting Act, which enabled the transfer of the rights and responsibilities of the company to the MS&LR.

A Line to Grimsby and the North Sea Docks

So far we have seen railways approach Doncaster from the south-east (GNR), the south-west and the north-east (SYR) but there is one further railway that was to play an important role in the town's development and this one emerged later than the others and from a north-westerly direction. The West Riding and Grimsby Railway promoted a line between Wakefield and Doncaster, with a short branch line connection from Adwick le Street to Stainforth, which gave access toward Grimsby. The company was promoted independently, but it was sponsored by the MS&LR and the GNR and became jointly owned by them.

The origins of this latest railway were born out of the frustration of the GNR's efforts to get a more direct line from Doncaster to Leeds. The GNR was authorized by Parliament in 1846 to build a railway line from London to York. Its promoters had hoped to be able to make a branch from Doncaster to Leeds, but that was refused by Parliament. Leeds and the surrounding district was a major centre of importance to the GNR, and to enable its trains to reach it, the GNR had to make agreements with other, competing, lines and run by a rather roundabout route via Knottingley and Methley.

The Bradford, Wakefield and Leeds Railway had been opened in 1857, and was worked by the GNR; this gave the GNR a direct line from Wakefield to Leeds, but the gap from Doncaster to Wakefield remained, necessitating running on the lines originally built the WP&GR, which were taken over by the Manchester and Leeds Railway in 1846, and the Lancashire and Yorkshire a year later.

The GNR was irked by having access to its West Riding interests only by courtesy of the Lancashire and Yorkshire Railway and had submitted Parliamentary bills seeking authorization for its own Doncaster to Wakefield line in 1857, 1860 and 1861. These had all been rejected, much to the chagrin of the company. To make matters worse, in 1861, a new company was promoted, to be called the West Riding and Grimsby Railway (WR&GR) and, much to the GNRs surprise, it was authorized on 7 August 1862. The logic of this apparent reversal of policy was that the line would give West Riding industries access to Grimsby docks, for export of their products. Although nominally independent, the project was sponsored by the SYR, with the active support of the MS&LR. The SYR was about to be leased by the MS&LR (and was from 1864) and could be regarded as under its influence in the interim. More worryingly for the GNR, the MS&LR was friendly toward the Great Eastern Railway (GER), which was trying to get access to the Yorkshire coal resources with a new trunk route from Cambridgeshire to Doncaster. This was a development that the GNR wished to prevent at all costs and probably motivated the company to take decisive action. It first tried to buy the WR&GR outright, but the ultimate control of this company was in the hands of the MS&LR which blocked the sale but suggested that an arrangement could be found for joint ownership. This wasn't much to the GNR's liking and it 'played for time' to see which way Parliament went with the GER's trunk route proposals. Parliament rejected these proposals in 1865 and suggested a joint ownership solution, which the GNR reluctantly had to accept was the only way it would get access to the Doncaster–Wakefield line. As part of the negotiated deal, the GNR gained access to the Stainforth–Grimsby section and the MS&LR access to GNR metals north-west of Wakefield. The joint ownership was agreed by Parliament in 1866, and immediately it came into effect, the GNR diverted all its London to Leeds trains on to the route, reducing the journey time by twenty minutes. This was probably considered by some contemporary observers as a high price to pay for the GNR, but the prize of the London to Leeds traffic by its route (now the quickest and most direct) was worth it.

The GNR/MS&LR joint line was not the only joint line serving Doncaster. With the GER's desire to access the Yorkshire to London coal traffic, and the rejection of its trunk route bill by Parliament in 1865, it now needed to consider its options. In 1863, the GER and the GNR had each submitted competing bills for a line from March to Spalding. The GNR bill was successful but the GER was awarded running rights over the new line, which can't have pleased the GNR board.

It was clear that a new approach was needed and, because of potential interests in Norfolk, the GNR needed to develop more friendly relations with the GER. It sensed that one of the GER attempts in Parliament must, eventually, be successful, so it offered the GER running powers for coal traffic from Gainsborough to Spalding. This was considerably less than the GER was seeking, so the GER suggested to the GNR that the two companies should be joint owners of the GNR loop-line between Spalding and Gainsborough, and of the GNR lines then under construction between Spalding and March, and Gainsborough and Doncaster.

As the GNR didn't reject this proposal out of hand, the GER sensed an opening and decided to build on the mood of constructive co-operation. In 1864, it proposed that the GNR build a new and direct joint line from Spalding to Lincoln through Sleaford. The GNR was receptive to this, saw that it would shorten the route of its loop-line through Boston and so a bill was prepared for the 1867 session of Parliament for the scheme. Unfortunately, the GER was in severe financial difficulty and was struggling to raise capital. In 1866, there was a national financial crisis when interest rates rose to 10 per cent in May. A new board was elected because of shareholder disquiet, but this new (GER) board had to face the fact that it was unable to raise capital, and there was not the remotest chance of finding the money that its predecessors had undertaken to pay the GNR. In fact, the GER had to find £1.5 million urgently to put its existing system in good order. The ensuing years were marked by a return to the old hostilities and, for the time being, joint railways were off the agenda.

The GER revived the proposal in 1872, but the GNR made demands that were far too high for the GER to agree, and once again the scheme lapsed, until discussions were re-opened in May 1876. This time the GNR proposed amalgamation, but the GER declined. In 1878, the GER was seriously considering the revival of the plan to build its own line through Sleaford and Lincoln to Askern. Just as the GER sought northward access to the coalfields, the GNR was desperate for an alternative route to relieve the main line and countered by depositing a fresh bill for a direct line from Spalding to Lincoln via Sleaford. Eventually common sense prevailed, and the two companies returned to Parliament. On 3 July 1879, the bill authorizing the joint line was passed. The GNR lines from Black Carr Junction (south of Doncaster) to Lincoln, and Spalding to March, the GER lines from Huntingdon to St Ives, from Needingworth Junction (near St Ives) to March, were all to be transferred to joint ownership. A new line was to be built from Spalding to Lincoln, and the junctions at Huntingdon and St Ives were to be improved. A joint committee was to be established to manage the line, and the GER was to pay the GNR £415,000, the difference in value of the respective lines becoming joint.

The route, affectionately known as 'the joint line', became a trunk artery for freight traffic, especially coal, with a large marshalling complex developed at Whitemoor, near March, for the sorting of wagons.

Doncaster Station

The original passenger station in Doncaster was a temporary affair constructed in 1849 as the terminus of the SYR. By arrangement, it also received traffic from the GNR Retford line when it opened in September of that year, just in time for the St Ledger meeting! Regular services started in November. The station at Cherry Tree Lane (later abbreviated to 'Cherrytree') was situated in the triangle of lines in Hexthorpe, where the SYR joined the GNR, about a mile south of the present station. Work began on a permanent station for the GNR at the location of the present station in 1850 and it was completed later that same year. Although owned by the GNR, the station was used by several railway companies by virtue of running powers and other agreements. These included the GNR from London and Lincoln to York, Leeds and beyond; the Midland Railway from Sheffield; the MS&LR from Wakefield and Grimsby; and the Lancashire and Yorkshire Railway from Manchester.

At the present time (2021), Doncaster is still a major railway 'hub' or meeting point with services operated by CrossCountry, East Midlands Railway, Hull Trains, TransPennine Express, Grand Central, Northern and LNER. This is the most train operating

THE PLANT

The very first locomotive works, known to railwaymen almost universally as 'The Plant', were established in the heart of the town centre in 1853 by the Great Northern Railway, transforming Doncaster from a peaceful Georgian market town into an engineering superpower. Over the years, many of the great names in railway design have been based here, including Patrick Stirling (designer of the Stirling Singles), H. A. Ivatt (designer of the Atlantic 4-4-2s for which he became famous), H. N. Gresley (later Sir Nigel), designer of the *Flying Scotsman* and the A4 Pacifics, all of which were built in The Plant.

Doncaster Station seen from the north on 25 May 1966 with ex-LNER Class A4 Pacific 4-6-2, 60024, Kingfisher, departing for the North. Although allocated to Aberdeen Ferryhill shed, the loco was less than four months from withdrawal, so its appearance so far south could have been in connection with a visit to the Plant (seen to the right of the loco) and was now being worked back to its home depot. JOHN HUNT

Ex-LNER A3 Pacific 4-6-2, 60107, Royal Lancer, speeds through Doncaster Station on the up fast line, on 12 May 1963, heading to London King's Cross and its home depot.
JOHN HUNT

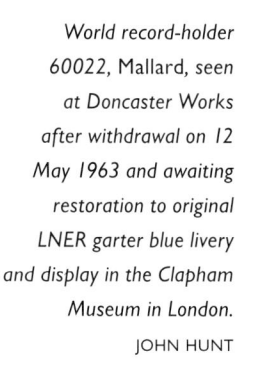

World record-holder 60022, Mallard, seen at Doncaster Works after withdrawal on 12 May 1963 and awaiting restoration to original LNER garter blue livery and display in the Clapham Museum in London.
JOHN HUNT

companies calling at any station in the UK, with the exception of Crewe, which has a similar number.

The original 1850 structure was substantially rebuilt in 1938 and now provides nine platforms on two islands: platforms 1, 3, 4 and 8 can take through trains; platforms 2 and 5 are south-facing bays; and 0, 6 and 7 are north-facing bays. In addition, the up and down main lines pass through the centre of the station.

In 1923, at the grouping of the railway companies, Doncaster became the main design centre for the LNER. Nigel Gresley had succeeded Ivatt as locomotive superintendent of the GNR in 1911 and from the grouping in 1923 became chief mechanical engineer of the LNER. Gresley, probably one of the most eminent locomotive engineers we have ever seen, was based at The Plant and designed the A1 Pacific, *Flying Scotsman*, which was exhibited at the British Empire Exhibition to represent the new LNER company and was the first steam locomotive to reach an authenticated 100mph.

In the 1930s, Gresley designed a new class of streamlined locomotives, the A4, also built in Doncaster, and chose one of them, *Mallard*, to chase the world speed record for a steam locomotive in 1938. *Mallard* reached 126mph (202km/h) – a record that remains to this day – and, in 2013, *Mallard* returned to the town where she was built to celebrate the 75th anniversary of that record.

Following the Grouping, the new company, the LNER, inherited the works of several of the constituent companies, notably Doncaster, York, Darlington, Inverurie and Stratford.

Doncaster remains an important railway town to this day and has been chosen to be the site of the new National College for High Speed Rail.

CHAPTER 5

Barnsley and the South Yorkshire Coalfield

Barnsley is home to three principal industries: linen-weaving, glass-making and coal-mining. The last became the most important and dominated the town's activity in the nineteenth and twentieth centuries, and the transport of the mineral shaped the development of transport infrastructure in this period.

Initial development came from the town's geographical position in the seventeenth century, when Barnsley developed into a stop-off point on the stage-coach route between Leeds, Wakefield, Sheffield and London. The traffic generated fuelled trade, with hostelries and related services prospering.

However, a much older industry, wire drawing, had been carried on since the time of James I and had the reputation of producing the best wire in the country. The industry declined in the late eighteenth century and was largely replaced, as an employer, by the manufacture of linen cloth. Barnsley became a centre for linen-weaving during the eighteenth and nineteenth centuries and grew into an important manufacturing town. The yarn was partly spun in large mills locally and partly brought from the mills of Leeds. It was mostly woven by the weavers in their own homes. About 1,000 power-looms and about 3,500 handlooms were employed and pure, clean water for bleaching, dyeing and powering machinery was available from the Sough Dyke and its tributaries. The population of Barnsley increased rapidly, rising from about 1,700 to almost 15,000 between 1750 and 1850.

Since the seventeenth century, there has also been a glass industry in the town, mostly concerned with the production of glass bottles. The industry still flourishes today in the twenty-first century and was noteworthy in the late nineteenth century for

OLD BARNSLEY

The first reference to Barnsley as a settlement occurs in 1086 in the Domesday Book, in which it is called Berneslai and had a population of around 200. The town developed little until it was given to the monks of Pontefract Priory, probably as some measure of compensation following their losses in the 'Anarchy' (the English and Norman Civil War that raged between 1138 and 1153). The monks built a town where three roads met: the Sheffield to Wakefield, Rotherham to Huddersfield and Cheshire to Doncaster routes. The original Domesday village became known as Old Barnsley, and a town grew up on the new site.

The monks established a market and, in 1249, a Royal Charter was granted to Barnsley permitting it to hold a weekly market on Wednesdays and an annual four-day fair at Michaelmas. Fifty years later, three annual fairs were being held. Despite being at the centre of the Staincross wapentake (a sub-division of the West Riding), it still had only 600 inhabitants in the mid-sixteenth century.

> **THE BARNSLEY COALFIELD**
>
> The coal found in the South Yorkshire Coalfield was a bituminous coal that was generally used to produce coal gas and coke. The coke was then used for iron and steel manufacture. Some seams produced coal suitable for raising steam, as it had a low ash and sulphur content. Finally, other seams produced coal for household use.
>
> The major seam in the South Yorkshire Coalfield was the Barnsley Seam. This seam, which was up to 10ft (3m) thick in places, provided a significant amount of the coal produced by this coal field. The Barnsley Seam coal properties varied through the depth of the seam: the top of the seam was a soft, bright coal; the middle section, known as the 'hards', was a dull, hard, high-quality coal suitable for raising steam; the bottom of the seam was another band of bright, soft coal called 'bottom softs'.

the invention of a sealable bottle to contain carbonated drinks by Hiram Codd at the Hope Glassworks.

Iron pits were to be found and an iron foundry was noted as early as 1380. Two ironworks opened in about 1795: Milton, which produced castings, and Elsecar producing pig-iron.

Notwithstanding all this industrial activity, the mining of coal easily exceeded them all in importance from the early nineteenth century onwards.

Water Highways

As observed in Chapter 1, transport by water was the only alternative to the pack horse. The need to transport ironstone, coal and an abundance of local limestone stimulated the development, in the late eighteenth century, of two strategic waterways and connecting tramways of varying gauges. With the Aire and Calder, Calder and Hebble and the Sheffield and South Yorkshire Navigations all within striking distance, there was much enthusiasm to tap into these potential traffic flows from the various collieries, iron pits and quarries that were springing up around Barnsley. In Chapter 4, we saw how the waterways in the area were improved by the opening of the Dearne and Dove Canal in 1804. With its two branches to Elsecar and Worsborough (now spelt Worsbrough), it facilitated the development and expansion of the mines along its route. From the basin in Worsborough (Worsbrough) a 3-mile (4.8km) tramroad to pits at Ratten Row, east of Thurgoland, was opened in about 1821. A 1½-mile (2.4km) branch from a junction at Rockly Smithies, to access coal and ironstone pits at Pilley, was opened in about 1832. The Worsborough Railway, as it became known, was built as a plateway of approximately 4ft 3in (1.29m) gauge and had a long life until finally abandoned in 1920.

The second branch of the Dearne and Dove (D&D) Canal terminated at Elsecar, from where a further 2¾-mile (4.4km) wagonway was constructed about 1837. Known as the Elsecar and Thorncliffe wagonway, it was constructed to serve the Milton Ironworks at Hoyland, the Thorncliffe Ironworks at Chappletown and several collieries and ironstone pits in the area. It was worked by a combination of stationary engines and horse haulage. The western section closed in 1879, and the inclined planes and stationary engines were taken out of use in 1880. The remainder was relaid as a standard-gauge colliery railway and came back into use in 1886 and lasted until about 1911.

The First Tramroads

The Barnsley Canal reached the town in 1799 and ran from a junction with the D&D Canal north of Barnsley to the Aire and Calder Navigation near Wakefield, a distance of about 14½ miles (23km). It was extended westwards for a further 3 miles (4.8km) to Barnby Basin in 1802. From this basin, a 2-mile (3.2km) tramroad was constructed to serve the coal pits at Silkstone village, opening in 1810. The gauge was about 4 ft (1.2m) and the rails were laid on very large stone blocks reportedly weighing more than 200lb (90kg) each. There were several short branches and, in 1830, the tramway was extended by a further 1¼ miles (2km) to serve pits at Silkstone Moor End. The entire railway was abandoned about 1860.

The development of these three early railways and the number of undertakings they served can be seen as indicative of an intense local expansion, the like of which had never been seen before. By the 1830s, an area stretching from Silkstone to Chapeltown came to be regarded as the most highly industrialized area in England. Thorncliffe Ironworks had an annual output of 7,000 tons (6,350 tonnes) of pig-iron, whilst Milton Ironworks was producing 3,200 tons (2,902 tonnes) of castings per year. Both Silkstone and Worsborough collieries could turn out 600 tons (544 tonnes) of high-quality coal per day when required.

Despite this, the coming of the railway age saw these industries decline quite quickly due to the inadequacy of the transport system. The Barnsley Canal achieved its maximum coal tonnage in 1839 and was then hit by the movement of rail-borne coal from County Durham.

So, for almost the first forty years of the nineteenth century, the waterway companies had the bulk carrying trade all to themselves. In 1840, the North Midland Railway (a later constituent of the Midland Railway) opened its Barnsley Station albeit at Cudworth, 2½ miles (4km) away on the NMR Derby to Leeds line. The arrival of this first railway was the 'writing on the wall' for waterway carrying and the chilly winds of competition started to erode its business. Coalmasters and ironmasters looked to the railway mania to provide some solutions to their need for speedier transport solutions.

The impossibly named Sheffield, Rotherham, Barnsley, Wakefield, Huddersfield and Goole Railway (SRBWH&GR) was formed in 1846 with the aim of providing access to the South Yorkshire coalfield. It was to link the Manchester and Leeds Railway (M&LR) from near Horbury, with the Sheffield and Rotherham Railway near Brightside, by way of Barnsley. Such was the pressure to gain access to the potentially lucrative traffic that, during the planning stage, the proposed railway was split in two at Barnsley: the northern portion being leased to the M&LR and the southern to the South Yorkshire, Doncaster and Goole Railway (SYD&GR). The Barnsley Exchange Station and the northern section opened first on 1 January 1850, with the southern section opening on 1 July 1851. Barnsley then became a through station, although the two sections of line were operated by different railways. On 1 July 1854, the Manchester, Sheffield and Lincolnshire Railway (MS&LR) opened a line from Penistone to Barnsley Exchange.

To provide a more convenient station for its Barnsley customers (closer than Cudworth), the Midland Railway (as the NMR had become) eventually opened a new line from Cudworth South Junction to Barnsley and a new, albeit temporary, station in Regent Street. The new station was made necessary due to the cramped conditions at Barnsley Exchange Station, with a single platform and three railway companies vying for space. The Midland Railway (MR) opened the line for goods traffic in April 1869 and for passengers on 1 May the following year, the delay being caused by a signalling dispute with the MS&LR over the connection at Pindar Oaks.

Passenger Stations

The MR set about building a new passenger station on the Regent Street site in an elevated position that was immediately west of Exchange Station, and in January 1872, completed the purchase of the Old Court House, which fronted on to Regent Street. The intention was to incorporate the building into its new station as a ticket office and waiting room. Thus, the new station was renamed Barnsley Court House Station. With an overall glass roof covering the two through platforms and its magnificent frontage, it was regarded as the most prestigious station in the area. There was also a short bay platform (No 3) at the Penistone end of the station. The new station opened for business on 23 August 1873.

The MS&LR, which had acquired the SYR, built a junction to the Midland line from Cudworth at Pindar Oaks, just to the east of the town. This gave it access to the Midland's new station and, on 1 June 1870, it moved its Doncaster to Barnsley passenger service there. The MS&LR also entered Barnsley from the Penistone direction and, by arrangement with the MR, constructed a junction, known as Court House

An interior view of Barnsley Court House Station seen in 1950. Working out its final years is 1895-built Midland Railway Johnson 1P 0-4-4T, 58075, on a local service to Cudworth. The loco would be withdrawn three years later, and the station closed in 1960.

Junction, from that line to the new station, enabling them to run a through service from Penistone to Doncaster. This meant that the company was the only one of the railways serving the town to operate a through service. Other services operated by the Midland to Court House and the Lancashire and Yorkshire to Exchange were stopping trains from Sheffield Midland, a shuttle service from Cudworth and the service from Wakefield, all terminating in the town.

The MS&LR provided goods facilities to the west of the passenger station, but its engine shed remained adjacent and to the east of Exchange Station with access over Jumble Lane crossing.

Despite the grouping of the private railway companies in 1923, Barnsley was still served by two of the 'big four' companies: the London and North Eastern Railway (LNER) and the London, Midland and Scottish Railway (LMSR). Barnsley Exchange, prior to the grouping, a Lancashire and Yorkshire

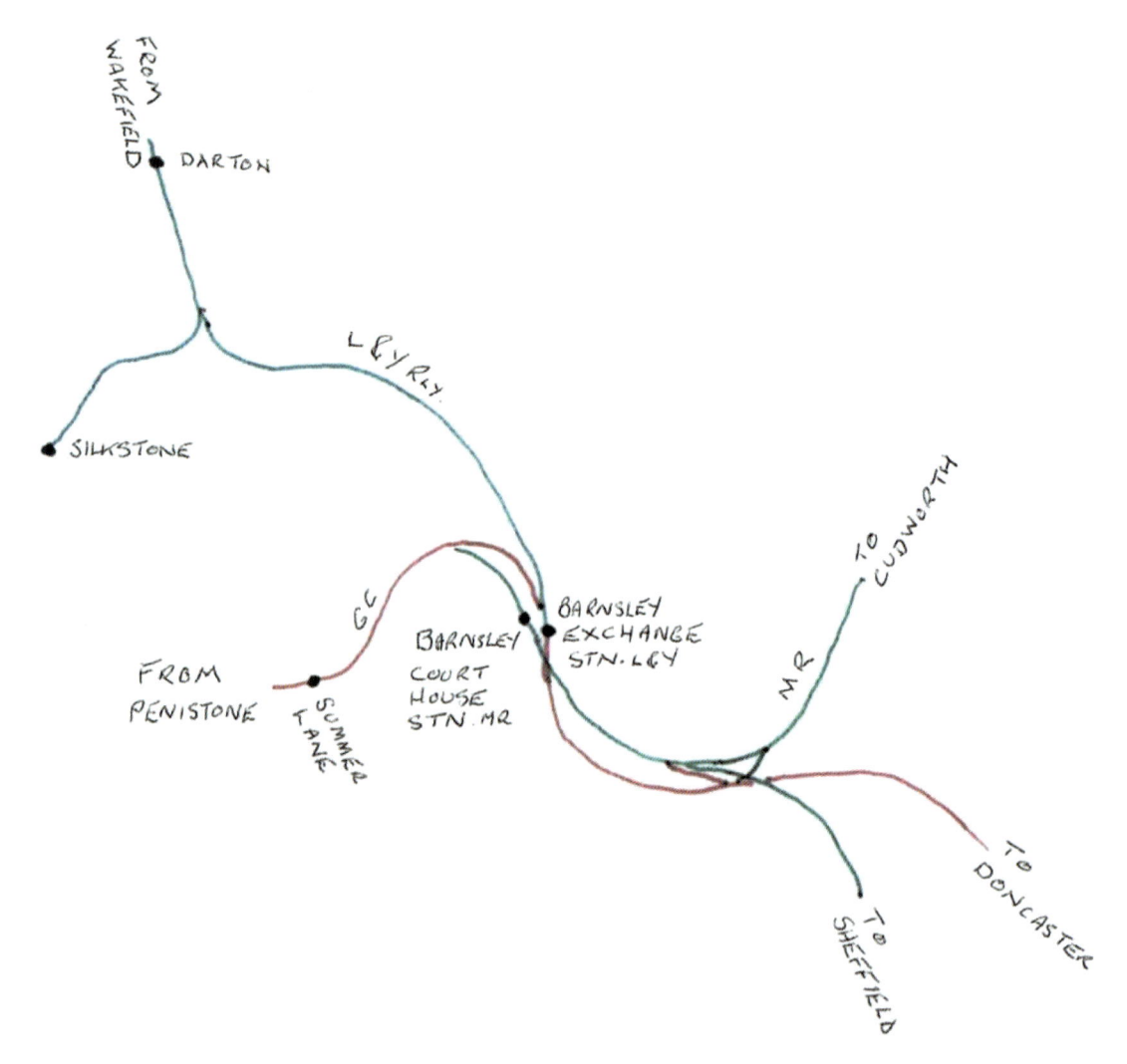

Railways around Barnsley in 1912.

owned station, became the LNER outpost and the Midland/Great Central (MSLR) Barnsley Court House became the opposing LMSR station.

Exchange Station is now the only station in Barnsley and has been renamed Barnsley Interchange, where a wide variety of bus services interconnect with the railway. There are three trains per hour to Leeds on Monday to Saturday – two are express services, calling only at Wakefield Kirkgate, whilst the third is an all-stations local that runs via Castleford. On Sundays, the service reduces to one express service and one stopping service to Leeds each hour. Two northbound Sunday services are extended to Carlisle. On the Penistone line, there is an hourly service northbound to Huddersfield seven days a week.

Southbound there are four trains per hour (two fast and two stopping). Two of these services terminate at Sheffield, whilst one fast train carries on to Nottingham and the other fast service runs through to Lincoln. The service drops to three per hour (one fast and two stopping) on Sundays.

Barnsley Court House Station hasn't fared so well. Services into the station were gradually reduced in the 1950s (although the Grand Central Railway (GCR) service from Wakefield via Nostell ended in September 1930), with the Cudworth service ending on 9 June 1958 and the Doncaster to Penistone service just over a year later, in June 1959. That left only the stopping trains from Sheffield Midland, which were re-routed to Barnsley Exchange from 19 April 1960, using a new curve at Quarry Junction from the Midland route on to the old SYR line from Sheffield Victoria. The station officially closed to passenger traffic the same day, although the last train had left four days previously.

In the early 1970s, the station was demolished and the Regent Street site used as a temporary home for Barnsley's open-air markets until a new market complex was completed. The Regent Street site has now become a car park with the Old Court House building in use as a pub/restaurant.

Demand for Coal

Barnsley, however, is synonymous with coal and for its coal mines. The Industrial Revolution created the demand for steam power to drive virtually anything mechanical: mills in both Lancashire and Yorkshire; factories all over the country engaged in the new manufacturing industry; coal and coal gas for cooking, heating and lighting; electricity generation; fuel for merchant shipping; not to forget coal for the steam locomotives that moved the raw material and finished product from mine to producer and to consumer. The early dominance of waterway transport soon gave way to the all-conquering railway companies. By 1880, there were fifty-one collieries within a 15-mile (24km) radius of Barnsley, all with access to the burgeoning railway network. Even in 1960, there were still seventy collieries within this radius, but the last of these closed in 1994.

For the rest of the nineteenth century and for most of the twentieth, the demand for coal was unremitting. Trainload after trainload poured out of the Yorkshire pits and formed the backbone of the railway companies' freight business and that of the nationalized railway industry.

To meet the sustained demand for coal, the mine owners were forced to go eastwards away from the shallow coal seams, sinking deeper shafts into the Barnsley Seam as it dipped downwards. By the turn of the twentieth century, many of the collieries on the exposed coalfield had exhausted the Barnsley Seam but, rather than abandon their investment and their experienced workforce, owners sank shafts through the all but exhausted Barnsley Seam into the Parkgate and Swallow Wood seams. Collieries such as Cortonwood, Manvers Main and Elsecar Main all fell into this category. Over to the east, these deep collieries in the concealed coalfield reached full production in the late 1920s and, in 1929, the South Yorkshire Coalfield achieved its highest output ever, producing 33.5 million tons (30.4 million tonnes) of coal, representing 13 per cent of UK output that year.

The first part of the twentieth century saw increasing competition in foreign markets and, thus, some mines were amalgamated to improve competitiveness. The long, slow decline of the industry was beginning. Technology away from the coalfield saw a gradual reduction in the size of the market as ships changed to oil as their principal fuel and many railways in the south of England were electrified. In 1938, the government nationalized the coal reserves, ostensibly to promote more efficient development of what was still considered a vital resource. The Second World War significantly increased demand for the fuel and, to ensure that production levels were met, conscript labour was redirected from the armed forces.

After the war, a Labour Government swept into power and very quickly fulfilled its manifesto pledge to take the coal mines into public ownership (along with the railways and road transport). For the next forty years, the National Coal Board managed the industry and, against a backdrop of increasing competition from abroad and a gradual decline in home demand, could carry out modernization and streamlining of production in a way that had not been seen in previous decades. This was achieved by closing inefficient and worked-out collieries,

Royston engine shed on a Sunday in July 1965. JOHN HUNT

Ardsley engine shed in July 1965. Note the loaded coal trains awaiting movement on the right of the picture. JOHN HUNT

and amalgamating and combining other collieries to form larger production units where significant assets, such as skip winders and coal washing and grading facilities, could be used by several collieries. The results of these actions, carried out against a backdrop of a volatile and declining market, was that by the time the collieries of South Yorkshire were sold to private owners at the end of the twentieth century, the coal they produced was some of the cheapest in the developed world.

LOCAL AUTHORITY COMMITMENT TO RAIL

Barnsley Metropolitan Borough Council has produced several rail strategies to try to bring about change. The latest, approved in November 2018, aims by 2033 to achieve the following:

1. Barnsley Station – removal of the Jumble Lane level-crossing and the resultant opportunity for station reconfiguration nearer to Barnsley Town Centre.
2. Deliver the Leeds–Sheffield Hallam line journey speed improvements to place Barnsley on the inter-city rail network map.
3. HS2 phase 2 eastern leg – confirmed provision of the HS2 South Yorkshire Parkway Station on the main HS2 eastern leg.
4. Inclusion of the Northern Powerhouse Rail (NPR) (Sheffield to Leeds and possibly part of Sheffield to Hull), including a new Dearne Valley Parkway Station.
5. Provide eastward connection from the Dearne Valley line to the East Coast Mainline (ECML), giving access to Doncaster and the Doncaster Sheffield Airport by using the ECML to Doncaster and the Doncaster–Lincoln line out of Doncaster to the proposed Doncaster Sheffield Airport Community Rail Station.
6. Barnsley services to be included in those having the new Class 195 and other high-quality rolling stock.
7. Improvements to station facilities and environs, including enhanced connections at Wombwell and Darton, improved parking facilities at Penistone and alternatives to existing steps at Wombwell and Elsecar.
8. Improvements to connectivity – increase in frequency throughout the network, specifically the introduction of two trains per hour between Huddersfield and Barnsley, alongside increasing the destinations served by the Barnsley network and levels of service in the peak hours and weekends.
9. Community Rail – explore with Community Rail partners the potential for reinstatement of passenger services on the former North Midland line from West Green to Wakefield and negotiate full support of DfT to local community rail partnerships when the soon expected future national Community Rail Strategy is confirmed.
10. Improved links to Rotherham and Doncaster.
11. Promote mass transit routes between Barnsley, Doncaster, Sheffield and Penistone (via Deepcar).

The Council is actively progressing the aspirations of this policy document and, already, Jumble Lane level-crossing has been closed, replaced by a temporary footbridge with approval given to the design of the permanent bridge due to be installed in late 2021. The future of Northern Powerhouse Rail and HS2 stage II will both influence the future direction of rail services in and around Barnsley.

To provide locomotives for the extensive coal traffic leaving the area, Barnsley had two steam sheds – Ardsley and Royston. They were grimy affairs with big, powerful, no-nonsense engines that rarely saw a cleaner from one year to the next. With the decline of steam traction, both depots closed soon after these pictures were taken: Ardsley in September 1965 and Royston in November 1967.

Despite this fiscal advantage, pits continued to close as the market for coal in the United Kingdom contracted with the development of gas-fired power stations, the continued use of cheap coal imports by power stations and the carbon tax. By January 2015, only two coal mines were still working: Kellingley and Hatfield Main. Hatfield closed in June 2015 and, on 18 December 2015, miners at Kellingley worked their final shift, marking the end of the United Kingdom's deep coal-mining industry.

The closure of coal mines in South Yorkshire (and Barnsley, in particular) had a very detrimental effect on the local economy. In areas where mining had been the sole employment opportunity, there was practically nothing to replace it. Deprivation was endemic, with unemployment levels approaching 50 per cent. Not only were the miners out of work, but all the ancillary businesses that contributed to daily life also suffered a high failure rate.

Whilst the core railway services to Leeds, Sheffield and Huddersfield survived, inter-city services did not. The standard of rolling stock declined relative to other more prosperous areas of the country.

CHAPTER 6

Sheffield and Rotherham

Sheffield is an important city in the south of the West Riding area. As we have seen, Leeds came to prominence as a centre for commerce from the Middle Ages onwards and seems to have assumed the role of capital of West Yorkshire. In the same way, Sheffield has made the most of the commercial opportunities brought about by the local coal, iron and gritstone deposits, becoming the 'uncrowned' capital of South Yorkshire.

Sheffield, a Short History

Sheffield was, reputedly, founded in the second-half of AD1 in a clearing by the River Sheaf, although there is evidence to suggest that humans have lived in the area for at least 10,000 years.

The name Sheffield has its origins in Old English and derives from the River Sheaf, whose name is a corruption of 'shed' or 'sheth', meaning to divide or separate. Field is a generic suffix deriving from the Old English 'feld', meaning a forest clearing. It is likely then that the origin of the present-day city of Sheffield is an Anglo-Saxon settlement in a clearing beside the confluence of the rivers Sheaf and Don, founded between the arrival of the Anglo-Saxons in this region (roughly the sixth century) and the early ninth century. Like so many towns in the West Riding, Sheffield grew and prospered because of its geography, but it took the advances in technology brought about by the Industrial Revolution to fully develop this prosperity. Natural resources, such as the fast-flowing rivers, already mentioned, plus the abundance of raw materials like coal, iron ore, ganister (a hard, fine-grained quartzose sandstone used in the manufacture of silica brick typically used to line furnaces) and millstone grit for grindstones found in the local hills, were all used in cutlery and blade production.

Most of this expansion of industrial activity took place in the eighteenth and nineteenth centuries, as shown by the massive rise in population. In 1736, Sheffield and its surrounding hamlets held about 7,000 people; in 1801, there were 60,000; and, by 1901, the population had grown to 451,195. Although the biggest expansion in trade came in this period, Sheffield had become a centre for blade production by the fourteenth century.

By 1600, Sheffield had become the biggest producer of cutlery outside London and, in 1624, the Company of Cutlers in Hallamshire was formed to oversee the trade. The eighteenth century was noteworthy for the development of new processes that would form the backbone of the industry. In the 1740s, Benjamin Huntsman, a clock-maker in the Sheffield suburb of Handsworth, had been fascinated with the production of steel in South and Central Asia in medieval times. He perceived that the production difficulty experienced by these early steel-makers could be attributed to their inability to melt the pig iron quickly enough with charcoal or coal. Benjamin Huntsman used coke rather than coal or charcoal, achieving temperatures high enough to melt steel and dissolve iron. Huntsman's process differed from some of the earlier processes in that it took a longer time to melt the steel and to cool it down, but allowed more time for the diffusion of carbon. Huntsman's process used iron and steel as raw materials, in the form of blister steel, rather than direct conversion from cast iron, as in puddling or the later Bessemer process. The ability to fully melt the steel removed any inhomogeneity in the steel, allowing the carbon to dissolve evenly into the liquid steel and negating the prior need for extensive blacksmithing in an attempt to achieve the same result. Similarly, it allowed steel to simply be poured into moulds, or cast, for the first time. The homogeneous crystal structure of this cast steel improved its strength and hardness in comparison with preceding forms of steel. The use of fluxes allowed nearly complete extraction of impurities from the liquid, which could then simply float to the top for removal. This produced the first steel of modern quality, providing a means of efficiently changing excess wrought iron into useful steel.

After serving a formal apprenticeship, Thomas Boulsover set himself up as a free cutler in the developing steel town of Sheffield. In early 1743, Boulsover made an accidental discovery that was to change his life and have an immense effect on the success and development of Sheffield. While repairing the decorative handle of a knife made from copper and silver, he accidentally slightly overheated the handle causing the two metals to fuse. Boulsover's initial despair at ruining a customer's expensive knife soon turned to elation when he realized the significance and potential of his find. Boulsover experimented with his discovery of Sheffield plate and found that when the silver and copper were fused together, they could be treated as one metal, meaning that an ingot of copper fused with a layer of silver could be rolled to any area and thickness and still retain the same proportion of the two metals. This satisfied Boulsover that the fused metal could be modelled into any article and could be used on a commercial scale. The product became known as Sheffield plate. Originally hand-rolled, old Sheffield plate was only used for making silver buttons. Then, in 1751, Joseph Hancock, previously apprenticed to Boulsover's friend Thomas Mitchell, first used it to make kitchen and tableware. This prospered and, in 1762–65, Hancock built the water-powered Old Park Silver Mills at the confluence of the Loxley and the Don, one of the earliest factories solely producing an industrial semi-manufacture. Eventually, old Sheffield plate was supplanted by cheaper electroplate in the 1840s. In March 1773, an Act of Parliament set up a silver assay office in Sheffield, bestowing the right to assay silver and issue its own hallmarks.

Huntsman's crucible process was only made obsolete in 1856 by Henry Bessemer's invention of the Bessemer converter. Despite this, production of crucible steel continued until well into the twentieth century for special uses, as steel from the Bessemer process was not of the same quality and mostly replaced wrought iron in such applications as rails. Bessemer tried tirelessly to persuade the various steel producers in Sheffield to take up his process, but to no avail. Eventually, he decided to undertake the exploitation of the process himself. He built his own steelworks in Sheffield and eventually demonstrated that he could produce steel for £20 a ton (0.91 tonnes), less than the indigenous steel-makers. Such a saving soon made the competition take notice!

In the early twentieth century, the search for a corrosion-resistant, non-tarnishing steel led, amongst other places, to the Sheffield laboratories of Brown Firth, where Harry Brearley discovered a means by which steel and chromium could be combined to make an alloy with the desired properties. Brearley's work was continued by his successor at Brown Firth, Dr William Hatfield. In 1924, he patented '18-8 stainless steel', which to this day is probably the most common alloy of this type.

Transport Systems Develop

For commerce to be successful there has to be an efficient transport system to bring in raw material and carry away the finished product. Unlike other towns in the West Riding, Sheffield was a late developer of transport systems. The Romans left a couple of roads when the occupation finished in AD410. After that it was not until the eighteenth century that improvements came about with the Turnpike Acts. In 1756, a turnpike to Chesterfield was constructed and, two years later, another one led to Buxton. Roads to Barnsley, Tickhill, Worksop, Intake and Penistone soon followed. The first railway was a 2-mile (3.2km) long wooden wagonway from the Duke of Norfolk's collieries at Tinsley Park and Manor into the town. This opened in 1774, but heavy wear on the wooden guide rails led to their replacement with L-shaped cast-iron rails to reduce the maintenance cost.

In common with other towns in the West Riding, Sheffield businessmen saw the River Don as a potential transport artery, but the upper reaches around the town were not navigable. In medieval times, goods from Sheffield had to be transported overland to the nearest inland port – Bawtry on the River Idle. An Act of Parliament to improve the navigation on the River Don was obtained by a group of Sheffield Cutlers in 1726. Over the next twenty-five years, locks and lock cuts were built and, by 1751, the river was navigable to Tinsley. To gain access to the waterway, an Act of Parliament was obtained on 7 June 1815 to bring into being the Sheffield Canal Company and to construct a canal 4 miles (6.3km) long from the River Don at Tinsley to the Sheffield Canal Basin (now Victoria Quays) in the city centre, passing through eleven locks. The original route suggested by the engineer William Chapman, although the cheapest solution, did not find favour with the principal backer, the Duke of Norfolk. He was concerned that the selected route did not allow access from his collieries at Tinsley Park and Manor, and as he was the principal shareholder, he could insist on a route more to his liking. To provide access to his Tinsley Park collieries, the 'Greenland Arm' was proposed. Less than three years after obtaining the Act, the canal was completed and it opened on 22 February 1819. The coming of the canal opened Sheffield to the large-scale transportation of freight. For nearly twenty years the canal company operated in almost monopolistic conditions, to the great delight of its shareholders.

The first railway to gain the attention of the Sheffield merchants was the North Midland Railway (NMR), which was in the planning stages in the early 1830s and would pass close to Rotherham. The engineer for this route was George Stephenson and he surveyed the line in 1835. As noted in Chapter 2, he had a horror of gradients steeper than 1 in 130 and so proposed to take the line east of Sheffield following the gentle gradients of the rivers Rother and Don, where the topography was also more favourable. The nearest the line was to come to Sheffield was Masborough, close to Rotherham. The Sheffield merchants made strong representations to the NMR and wheeled out railway celebrities Joseph Locke, Charles Vignoles and George Hudson to convince Stephenson to bring the line through Sheffield. However, Stephenson was not convinced, and he routed the NMR via the Rother Valley.

Fearful that the town would be marginalized, a group of Sheffield merchants, including two Coal Masters, proposed a short, 5-mile (8km) long railway from a station at Wicker in Sheffield to Westgate in Rotherham. The proposed railway was to cross the route of the North Midland at Masborough, before crossing the River Don and entering Rotherham. The Act for the incorporation of the Sheffield and Rotherham Railway (S&RR) received the Royal Assent on 4 July 1836, with the North Midland also being approved on the same day.

Construction of the line proceeded quickly and, although the earthworks were unfinished and the second track had not been laid, the railway opened on 31 October 1838. The line was an instant success and the number of passengers in the first year was double that which had been predicted when the line was put before Parliament. With the North Midland nearing completion in 1840, the S&RR built a short branch northwards to connect with it at Masborough Station in time for the opening on 1 July. At a board meeting the previous February, the S&RR agreed terms for the NMR to operate a service from Leeds to Sheffield, obviating the need for a change at Masborough. This service was introduced as soon as the NMR opened through to Leeds in July 1840.

Despite the promising early results, the economic stagnation of 1841 and 1842 meant that the S&RR saw little profit in the following years. In January 1843, the line's only intermediate station, Grimesthorpe Bridge, closed.

Other prospective railway companies had Sheffield in their sights and the Sheffield, Ashton-under-Lyne and Manchester Railway (SA&MR) was opened in stages from west to east between 1841 and 1845, and gave Sheffield its first main-line station at Bridgehouses. This was a railway with some fearsome challenges to be overcome in its construction. The gradients were severe and the line crossed the Pennine ridge by way of the infamous Woodhead Tunnel. This was over 3 miles (4.8km) long and located in very inhospitable country. Contemporary accounts suggest that little provision for living accommodation for the 'navvies' was made, with many of them living out in the open, even in the depths of winter, using stone shelters to provide some respite from the elements. Later in the project, the company relented and purchased 400 tents! The tunnel was a single-line bore, built on a gradient of 1 in 201 rising toward the east. When completed, the first Woodhead Tunnel was one of the world's longest railway tunnels at 3 miles 13yd (4,840m). It was the first trans-Pennine tunnel to be built, preceding the Standedge and Totley Tunnels, which are slightly longer. The tunnel had cost roughly £200,000 (equivalent to £19,930,000 in 2020) to build. The human cost was high: thirty people lost their lives, 200 workers were maimed and 450 suffered some form of injury in the harsh working conditions. None the less, the opening of the route, in 1845, gave access to new markets for Yorkshire coal in the burgeoning industries of Lancashire.

Of great significance was a meeting on 5 September 1845 between the SA&MR, the Great Grimsby and Sheffield Junction Railway and the Grimsby Docks Company. The outcome was an agreement to amalgamate the three concerns, forming a single railway connecting Manchester and Grimsby. The idea was developed and approved by Parliament on 27 July 1846, to be effective on 1 January 1847. The combined company would be named the Manchester, Sheffield and Lincolnshire Railway (MS&LR) and the original SA&MR line was extended to a new station, Sheffield Victoria, in 1851.

Railway Competition 'Hots Up'

The state of the money market considerably improved in 1844–45 and what later became known as the railway mania took hold. The directors of the S&RR bravely decided, in February 1844, that expansion regardless of cost was the only way to protect itself. A start was made, in 1847, by the construction of a small connecting line with SA&MR at Bridgehouses. This was a short, steeply graded line, enclosed almost entirely within a tunnel.

With the recession fading away in 1843 and the Midland Railway being created on 10 May 1844 by the Great Midland Amalgamation Bill, the S&RR wasted no time in beginning negotiations with the new company for either sale or lease of its railway to the MR. Terms were agreed quickly and the MR started operations over the S&RR on 10 October 1844. The title of S&RR existed on paper until the takeover was finally authorized by an Act of Parliament on 21 July 1845.

The Great Northern Railway was keen to be able to access Sheffield but, despite two attempts to gain Parliamentary approval for a line from Retford, had had to be content with running powers over the MS&LR. In 1850, it notified this company that it intended to introduce a Lincoln to Sheffield service from 7 August. This date coincided with the completion of the GNR line into London and was probably intended as a 'wake-up call' to the Midland to improve on its existing Sheffield to London service via Masborough. It was to be another twenty years before the Midland was to open the direct line to Derby via Dronfield.

Running from the Hope Valley, a pair of unidentified BR Class 25 locos head a block freight service out of Totley Tunnel, Sheffield, in May 1979. JOHN HUNT

The GNR's ultimate aim was a route from London to Manchester and it achieved this on 1 August 1857, with the introduction of the 'Manchester Flyers' covering the 203 miles (326km) from King's Cross to London Road in five hours twenty minutes and quickly cut to an even five hours. Great Northern locomotives ran as far as Sheffield.

In 1870, the MR recognized the need for a more direct route to the south from Sheffield and opened a diversion from the NMR line through Dronfield to Sheffield, which became known to railwaymen as the 'new road', as opposed to the 'old road'. It followed a route that, in 1840, would have been uneconomic to build and difficult to work. Nevertheless, the terrain was more difficult than for the other two railways to Derby, requiring 200 bridges, seven tunnels and an aqueduct for the railway to pass underneath the Cromford Canal. This diversion passed through a new station in Sheffield (Pond Street) replacing the S&RR facility at Wicker. Some historians claim that from the opening in 1870, the station was referred to as Sheffield (Pond Street) and was renamed Sheffield (Midland) when extensions and improvements were carried out in 1905. It is understood that, although Pond Street can be found on some MR maps, it was never used in the company's timetables or referred to locally by this name. The author believes that the 'Midland' name was used from the beginning. Most of the original North Midland line and the Sheffield diversion are still in use today.

Another railway to have a bearing on the development of railway services in and around Sheffield was the grandly titled Lancashire, Derbyshire and East Coast Railway (LD&ECR). Its purpose was to link the coalfields of Nottinghamshire and

Derbyshire with Warrington and a new port on the Lincolnshire coast. It was a huge undertaking, and the company was unable to raise the money to build its line. However, with the financial help of the Great Eastern Railway (GER), it managed to open between Chesterfield and Lincoln with a branch toward Sheffield from 1896. Showing considerable strategic planning, the GER supported the LD&ECR in return for running powers over its route and the access to the coalfields this would bring. The cash-strapped nature of the company meant that the Sheffield branch was not completed, only reaching Barlborough Colliery.

However, the LD&ECR had a long-held ambition to reach Sheffield, but running powers over the MS&LR from Beighton were consistently refused. As well as the GER (which sought the access too), independent business interests in the town urged some means of making a connection. A first attempt at a semi-independent line to Sheffield, in April 1894, failed, as the LD&ECR was, as we have seen, strapped for cash. A second application to Parliament, in 1896, was more successful and resulted in an Act of Parliament dated 4 August 1896 for the Sheffield District Railway. This would be a new line running from the LD&ECR at Spink Hill, on the Beighton branch, to a new terminus, Attercliffe, in Sheffield. The company was backed by the GER and the LD&ECR, both of which would have running powers; the LD&ECR would work the line for 50 per cent of the gross receipts.

With an eye to the future, the MR offered access over its own line into Sheffield and suggested the LD&ECR make a junction with the MR at Killamarsh and have running powers to Treeton over the MR. From there it could build its own line to Brightside, joining the MR Rotherham line and have running powers from there to a point close to the intended Attercliffe terminal. As a final sweetener, the MR offered running powers to its main passenger station in Sheffield. For a railway that had always known hard times, this was an attractive offer, saving 6 miles (9.6km) of new construction but set at the cost of a more roundabout route. Any qualms were quickly overcome; the MR offer was accepted and construction quickly started.

In 1897, construction of the LD&ECR Beighton branch north-westwards from Barlborough Colliery Junction was in progress with the 501yd (451m) Spink Hill Tunnel being the chief engineering feature. The variation of the authorized route was passed by Act of Parliament dated 12 August 1898.

The branch was brought into use for coal and goods traffic from Barlborough Colliery Junction to a new LD&ECR station at Killamarsh, a distance of 4½ miles (7.2km), together with an intermediate station at Spink Hill, on 21 September 1898, and for all traffic on 1 October 1898. Its extension to the connection with the MR at Killamarsh (Beighton Junction), a further 1½ miles (2.4km), was opened on 29 May 1900 for goods traffic and the following day for passengers. The GER got access to Sheffield through its running powers' agreement with the LD&ECR, a considerable benefit to that company, cheaply obtained. Hopes of reaching the Lincolnshire coast were never fulfilled and the LD&ECR's dependency on other lines limited its future. It was, however, able to operate the passenger service on the Sheffield District Railway (SDR), although the MR later ran passenger trains too. The SDR did not have rolling stock and did not operate trains itself. The LD&ECR was absorbed by the GCR in 1907, and the GCR inherited the LD&ECR running powers.

The provision of rail freight facilities in the Sheffield area had grown piecemeal over more than a hundred years and had been developed by many individual railway companies. By 1961, when a tenth of rail-borne freight in Britain originated in the Sheffield area, British Railways sought central government funding to rationalize and improve facilities for freight handling.

The Giant Marshalling Yard

The result was the Sheffield district rail rationalization plan, which set out to replace most marshalling yards in the Sheffield area with one large yard at

Tinsley. The government's central economic planning and economic self-sufficiency policy saw the situation as a major limit on Britain's economic growth and enabled the plan to receive financial support. A location on the Sheffield District line was chosen, which gave good access to both the former MR and former GCR networks in the area. Work started in 1963, with new connections being built at Treeton, Broughton Lane and Tinsley South. The location allowed easy access to the brand new central Sheffield freight terminal at Grimesthorpe and the new Freightliner terminal on the site of the Masborough Sorting Sidings in Rotherham, one of the many yards that Tinsley replaced. The yard opened in 1965.

As part of the national freight plan, Tinsley was to be a major network yard where wagon-load freight trains would arrive, be split and sorted into new trains for onward departure to other network yards; directly to the many rail-connected businesses in the area in 'trip' freights; or to the freight terminal for unloading and forwarding by road. To assist with this, it featured gravity-assisted shunting and a new computerized system of wagon control, as developed in the USA.

At the time of opening, the yard was handling 3,000 wagons a day. Incoming trains were split in the eleven reception sidings, propelled over the hump in the yard, from where the individual wagons rolled down a slope and were automatically sorted into new trains on the yard's fifty main sorting sidings. The yard had its own dedicated class of shunting locomotive (BR Class 13) for this purpose, as BR's standard class of shunting locomotive was not considered to be powerful enough. Each of the main sorting sidings was fitted with computer-controlled retarders to either slow down the rolling wagons before they hit other wagons already on the siding, or give wagons rolling too slowly a boost to move them along to the correct position in a particular siding. This wagon-control system, manufactured by Dowty, was very complex, needed almost constant maintenance and, crucially, could not handle the longer wheelbase wagons that were already becoming prevalent and required individual shunting. In addition, there was an express freight and departure yard of ten sidings and a twenty-five-road secondary yard for local freight trains (with its own hump).

In 1965, the electrified Manchester–Sheffield–Wath line (the Woodhead Route) was extended into the yard to allow electrically hauled trains to and from the Manchester area to be handled. Seventeen miles of track from Woodburn Junction and Darnall Junction via Broughton Lane to the Reception Sidings at Catcliffe were electrified at 1500V DC. Unlike similar electrified marshalling yards, to save on costs, the main body of the sorting sidings was not electrified: a half of the arrival sidings was electrified for incoming electric trains; departing electric trains either had to use the southern third of the main sorting sidings (the western part of which were wired for electric trains) or had to be drawn out of the main sorting sidings by diesel locomotives into electrified departure roads where the electric locomotives were attached.

From an early stage, the yard was not used to its full capacity: by the late 1960s, road competition was biting hard into the railways' goods traffic and, in particular, the wagon-load freight that required hump-yards like Tinsley was already declining. The economic malaise and industrial decline of the 1970s exacerbated this. By the 1980s, British Rail was closing its remaining wagon-load freight facilities as being uneconomic.

In 1981, the electrification in the yard was removed with the closure of the Manchester–Sheffield–Wath system. On 17 December 1984, the arrival sidings and hump were closed, the wagon-control system removed and the remaining Class 13s scrapped. The yard connections were relaid to allow easier handling of block-load trains, which now dominated rail freight in Britain. By 1995, the decline in British heavy industry meant that this type of traffic had also declined massively, resulting in the closure of the locomotive depot on 27 March 1998. The eastern connections (both north- and south-facing chords) to the Midland 'Old Road' were closed in 1992. However, the track is still in situ, and the western

Standing in Sheffield Midland Station with a special train, on 4 September 1965, is Peppercorn A1 Pacific 4-6-2, 60145, St Mungo (nameplates removed). The number of photographers on the track and the bowler-hatted gentleman clearing the way, suggest that this was no ordinary special! The 60145 was a York engine at this date. JOHN HUNT

connection to the Midland Main Line (and goods depot at Grimethorpe) at Brightside junction was lifted in 1999. Both chords to the ex-MS&LR/GCR line from Woodburn to Rotherham (via Broughton Lane junction and Tinsley South junction) remain open. The rest of the yard progressively fell into disuse over the next ten years.

A few years later only the main sorting sidings remained: a part of these were to be used to stable steel trains destined for the Sheffield area; the rest of the remaining sidings were used to store surplus-to-requirements rolling stock in a poor state of repair. However, in 2007 the remaining sidings were lifted and a new, much smaller yard laid, additionally a new rail-linked distribution and goods transsshipment centre – Sheffield International Rail Freight Terminal (SIRFT) – was constructed.

Between 1840 and 1870, no less than five stations had been opened in Sheffield. However, by then the passenger railway network in the Sheffield area had largely been completed and the stations rationalized. The five stations were:

A night-time view of Sheffield Midland Station on 18 November 1967 with BR Standard Class 5 4-6-0, 73069, heading a north-bound service. JOHN HUNT

1. Wicker, 1840–70. Built by the S&R Railway, taken over by the MR in 1845. Replaced by Pond Street/Midland in 1870.
2. Bridgehouses 1845–51. Built by the Sheffield and Rotherham Railway. Constituent of the MS&LR formed in 1847 but replaced by Victoria Station in 1851.
3. Victoria 1851–1970. Built by MS&LR which became the GCR in 1897 and was grouped into the LNER in 1923.
4. Pond Street 1870–1905. Built by the MR. Became:
5. Midland 1905 to date. MR grouped into the LMS in 1923.

With two major stations serving the city (Victoria and Midland) a comprehensive range of destinations were available as follows:

- From Sheffield Victoria – Although subsequently closed, the 1950s saw the station at its zenith being used by regular Manchester London Road–Sheffield Victoria–London Marylebone expresses by the Great Central route and London King's Cross over the East Coast Main Line via Retford. Named expresses using the station included the *Master Cutler*, the *Sheffield Pullman* and the *South Yorkshireman*. There were also many semi-fast trains running trans-Pennine from Manchester to destinations on the East Coast

Sheffield area railways 1931.

and local trains to Chesterfield, Barnsley, Nottingham, Doncaster, Retford, Penistone and Lincoln.
• From Sheffield Midland – Express services south to Derby, Birmingham and the West Country; to London via the Midland Main Line (and the East Coast Main Line following the closure of Victoria); express services to the north to Leeds, Carlisle and Glasgow; to Doncaster, York, Newcastle and Edinburgh; to Hull and to Cleethorpes, Mablethorpe and Skegness.

The Beeching cuts led to the closure of the Great Central route to London Marylebone in 1966, followed by the Woodhead line to Manchester Piccadilly in 1970. These closures made Victoria Station virtuously obsolete, closure coming on 5 January 1970. The station buildings were demolished in 1989, leaving only the Wicker Arches, on which it stood, remaining, and carrying the freight-only line to Deepcar steel works, between Oughtibridge and Stocksbridge.

CHAPTER 7

Airedale and Wharfedale

Airedale

Part of the Yorkshire Dales, Airedale is a river valley or dale formed by the River Aire. It stretches from the river's origin in Aire Head Springs, Malham, down past Skipton on to Keighley, Bingley and Shipley, through to Leeds and Castleford to join the River Ouse at Airmyn. Known as the Aire Gap, the valley is of great topographic significance in that it provides low-altitude passes through the mid-Pennines to the west coast. This became the 'route of choice' for George Stephenson when he was asked to survey the area and suggest a route for a railway to link Leeds and Bradford in 1843. Thus, the Leeds and Bradford Railway (L&BR), after obtaining an authorizing Act of Parliament in July 1843, opened on 1 July 1846 with stations at Wellington Street (Leeds) and in Bradford at the bottom of Kirkgate, known simply as 'Bradford'. Stephenson routed the line up the Aire Valley to Shipley and then turned south and followed Bradford Dale to Bradford – the only reasonably flat approach to the town.

The presence of the Bradford Canal, opened in 1774, had led to the partial industrialization of towns in the Aire Valley, such as Keighley, Bingley and Skipton. The railway proprietors could see a future stream of ready business along this route and, indeed, the 1843 Act had foreseen the potential for an extension to Bingley and Keighley. No time was lost with this new venture and an Act, entitled 'The Leeds and Bradford (Shipley–Colne Extension) Railway Act of 30 June 1845' was obtained. Note the extension beyond Skipton into Lancashire at Colne. The Act empowered the company to build its line as an extension of the L&BR, which was still under construction.

The line began at a triangular junction with the L&BR at Shipley and the first section was from there to Keighley. A contract for the construction was let on 15 October 1845 and the section opened to passengers on 16 March 1847. The line included a 151yd (138m) tunnel at Bingley. The section from Keighley to Skipton was also being constructed at much the same time and was opened about six months later, on 7 September 1847. This was initially a single-track affair, presumably to reap some income from the investment made, but by the end of the year it had been doubled. Trains ran between Bradford and Skipton; passengers to and from Leeds changed at Shipley.

The contract for the construction of the final section from Skipton to Colne was let on 9 September 1846 and was opened to traffic on 2 October 1848. The intention at Colne was to make an end-on junction with the, under construction (and snappily titled), East Lancashire Railway's 'Blackburn,

Although its status as a continuing part of the nation's railway system had been confirmed some twenty years previously, this positivity had yet to extend to the standard of passenger rolling stock employed. When the Midland Railway opened the route, there were direct trains between London and Glasgow, many with Pullman accommodation. However, by the date of this picture (2010) services had been taken over by the mundane Class 158 DMU and we see Northern Rail 158902 easing into platform 3 at Skipton with the 08:53 Carlisle to Leeds Service on Tuesday 10 August 2010.

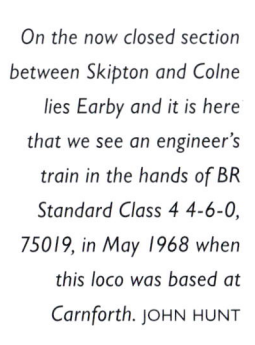

On the now closed section between Skipton and Colne lies Earby and it is here that we see an engineer's train in the hands of BR Standard Class 4 4-6-0, 75019, in May 1968 when this loco was based at Carnforth. JOHN HUNT

Burnley, Accrington and Colne Extension Railway'. This was completed and opened on 1 February 1849 and by 2 April the line had become part of a through route between Leeds and Liverpool, although most passenger trains were locals between Skipton and Colne. In July 1846, the Leeds and Bradford Extension Railway (L&BER) was leased by the Midland Railway and absorbed by that company on 24 July 1851.

The route now established up the Aire Valley facilitated other railway company promotions. The 'little' North Western Railway (NWR) was one of them. The correct title of the company was the North Western Railway Company. However, to avoid confusion with the much larger London and North Western Company, the descriptive word 'little' was commonly used as a prefix. The NWR was incorporated on 26 June 1846 to build a railway from Skipton on the L&BER to Low Gill on the Lancaster and Carlisle Railway. The purpose was to carry Yorkshire-to-Scotland rail traffic. Included in the authorizing Act was a branch from the Yorkshire town of Clapham to Lancaster, where an end-on junction with an associated company, the Morecambe Harbour and Railway Company, was planned. This company had been incorporated on 16 July 1846 to build a harbour on Morecambe Bay. The location was close to the village of Poulton-le-Sands and included in the Act was a 3-mile (4.8km) railway to Lancaster, where a new station at Green Ayre was proposed. The single-track line opened on Whit Monday, 12 June 1848. To complete the connection with the NWR, a short connecting curve to Lancaster Castle, on the Lancaster and Carlisle Railway, was opened on 18 December 1849. The company amalgamated with the NWR within months of its incorporation, although technically it remained a separate company until absorption by the MR on 1 June 1871.

The original NWR 'main line' opened between Skipton and Ingleton on 31 July 1849. However, due to an economic recession, work on the Ingleton to Low Gill section was suspended, so the NWR was forced to concentrate on the branch to Lancaster. Soon after, the line eastwards along the Lune Valley from Lancaster Green Ayre to Wennington opened on 17 November 1849. The line extended further east to Bentham by 2 May 1850 and, finally, to Clapham on 1 June 1850, where it joined the already completed line from Skipton. A horse bus had been used to bridge the gap between Wennington and Clapham during construction.

Upon completion of the Morecambe to Skipton line, the Clapham to Ingleton section was closed by the cash-strapped NWR, just ten months after opening, as the prospect of completing the partly built branch to Low Gill seemed remote.

The whole line was originally single track but, by 1850, the Hornby to Hellifield section had been doubled. Three years later this was extended to Skipton. However, Morecambe to Lancaster remained single track until 1877 and Lancaster to Hornby until 1889. The curve between the two Lancaster stations was never doubled.

With a strategic eye on its future Anglo-Scottish traffic, the MR had been a close collaborator with both the NWR and Morecambe Harbour and Railway Company (MH&R). From 1 June 1852, the NWR was worked by the MR. Seven years later, on 1 January 1859, both the NWR and the MH&R were leased to the MR and, on 30 July 1874, the NWR was absorbed by the MR.

Despite the NWR being unable to construct the section of line between Ingleton and Low Gill, others were casting covetous eyes upon it. Backed by the mighty London and North Western Railway (L&NWR), the Lancaster and Carlisle Railway was authorized, in 1857, to take over construction of the abandoned Ingleton to Low Gill line. Four years later, the line opened to passengers on 16 September 1861 but, inconveniently, although physically connected at Ingleton, the lines were not logically connected, as the L&NWR and Midland could not agree on sharing the use of Ingleton Station. Instead, the L&NWR terminated its trains at a new station at the end of Ingleton Viaduct. Midland Railway passengers had to change on to L&NWR trains by means of a walk of about a mile over steep gradients between the two stations. However, by 1862, the two companies' differences were partly

Trespass on the railway to see A3 Pacific 4-6-2, 4472, Flying Scotsman, is no twenty-first century phenomenon. This picture dates back to 4 September 1965 and shows the celebrity locomotive (by then in private ownership and repainted into LNER green livery) at Yorkshire's Clapham Junction with an enthusiast's special train bound for Low Gill and Carlisle. JOHN HUNT

resolved and L&NWR trains began to run through to the Midland station. However, the Midlands' rights of access to L&NWR tracks toward Scotland were difficult to enforce. Despite the agreement enabling the Midland to attach through carriages to L&NWR trains at Ingleton, which enabled passengers to continue their journey north without leaving the train, the situation was still not ideal, as the L&NWR handled the through carriages of its rival with deliberate obstructiveness, for example, by attaching the coaches to slow goods trains instead of fast passenger workings.

The Midland board decided that the only solution was a separate route to Scotland. Surveying began in 1865 and, in June 1866, Parliamentary approval was given to the Midland's bill for the Settle to

Another view of the Clapham Station area on 12 June 1967 showing BR Standard Class 4, 4-6-0, 75039 working a train of track materials recovered from the demolition of the line to Low Gill. The loco was based at Tebay shed at this time but within three months had been withdrawn and sent for scrap, after only fourteen years' service. At the other end of the yard is Lostock Halls ex-LMS 8F 2-8-0, 48510 with a similar train. This loco was scrapped the following January but had racked up 24½ years' service. JOHN HUNT

Carlisle Railway. Soon after, the Overend–Gurney banking failure sparked a financial crisis in the UK. Interest rates rose sharply, several railways went bankrupt and the Midland's board, prompted by a shareholders' revolt, began to have second thoughts about a venture where the estimated cost was £2.3 million (equivalent to £210m in 2020). As a result, in April 1869, with no work started, the company petitioned Parliament to abandon the scheme it had earlier fought for. However, Parliament, under pressure from other railways that would benefit from a scheme that would cost them nothing, refused. The Midland was, therefore, obliged to commence construction, which it did in November of that year.

The engineer for the project was John Crossley from Leicestershire, a veteran of other Midland schemes. The terrain traversed is among the bleakest and wildest in England and construction was halted for months at a time due to frozen ground, snowdrifts and flooding. This meant that the time to construct was extended, as was the cost, which rose to £3.6 million (equivalent to £340m in 2020) – 50 per cent above the estimate and a colossal sum for the period. The line opened for goods traffic in August 1875, with the first passenger trains starting in April 1876 and an official opening on 1 May 1876. As part of the MR's main line from London, St Pancras to Carlisle, Citadel and on to Glasgow, St Enoch, the L&BER to Skipton and the 'little' North Western from Skipton to Hellifield and Settle Junction, became part of an important and busy main-line railway.

With the elevation to the status of a main-line railway, many improvements to keep pace with the developing and increasing traffic flow were

For the provision of locomotives, Skipton was a key location. The Midland Railway opened a shed here in 1877, shortly after the opening of the Settle to Carlisle Railway a year earlier. The demands for motive power over this route were heavy and arduous, with a mixture of heavy coal trains and express passenger services to cater for. During the winter months, keeping the line open in snowy conditions was no mean feat; a snow plough can be seen in the centre of this picture, which dates from September 1965. Most of the work undertaken by the shed was local passenger trains for which Midland 3F and 4F locos were provided. JOHN HUNT

The Settle and Carlisle Railway has remained popular for scenic excursion trains, particularly if they are steam-hauled. In this image, from August 2009, LMS Jubilee Class 4-6-0 5690, Leander, is storming through Settle Station as it gets into the long climb (averaging 1 in 100) to Blea Moor summit, a distance of 16 miles (26km).

TRAINS FOR THE WOOL BARONS

Many barons of the wool industry did not live where their wealth was created. The air was too sooty from all the mill chimneys and they preferred coastal locations where the air was cleaner. To cater for this, residential specials were put on in the mornings running from Morecambe to Bradford and returning in the evenings. In the 1920s, two club cars were included in the formation of these trains so that the wool magnates could socialize with their own kind and enjoy appropriate liquid refreshment!

made. Between 1896 and 1910, the section between Leeds and Shipley was gradually quadrupled. This included a flyover at Kirkstall to take the Leeds–Bradford 'fast' lines over the 'slow' lines, which mainly carried freight from Leeds and the south to Scotland. Benefits also accrued to the towns along this main-line railway corridor. Keighley and Skipton grew rapidly in the 1870s and the pace of industrialization quickened.

Local services were taken over by diesel multiple units (DMUs) on 5 January 1959, but these were withdrawn on 22 March 1965 (as a result of the 'Beeching axe') when all intermediate stations,

With the quadrupled track layout clearly on display, ex-LMS Class Class 4P 2-66-4T 42638 heads a short train, running under clear signals, approaches Shipley, bound for Bradford in February 1967. JOHN HUNT

Preserved ex-LMS 8F 2-8-0, 48431, heads a train out of Keighley on the Worth Valley line June 1995. The line was the former Midland Railway branch from Keighley to Oxenhope.

Siemens-built Northern Rail Class 333 EMU, 333007, waits at Skipton for its next turn of duty down the Aire Valley line to Leeds on 10 August 2010.

Northern Rail Class 142 Pacer, 142096, arrives at Skipton with the 10:19 Leeds to Heysham Port service on Tuesday 10 August 2010.

except Shipley, Bingley and Keighley, were closed. The Leeds to Bradford passenger workings were transferred to the Stanningly route on 1 May 1967 and the 'fast' lines from Armley to Thackley were closed on the same date. Some of the closed stations, such as Saltaire, were re-opened during the 1980s.

In 1994, the line was electrified at 25kV AC overhead between Leeds and Skipton, and new British Rail Class 333 trains were introduced in the early 2000s. Investment in the line has seen passenger numbers grow, and now overcrowding on trains is a problem.

Wharfedale

Wharfedale is the upper valley of the River Wharfe. Towns and villages in Wharfedale (downstream, from west to east) include Buckden, Kettlewell, Conistone, Grassington, Hebden, Bolton Abbey, Addingham, Ilkley, Burley in Wharfedale, Otley, Pool-in-Wharfedale, Arthington, Collingham and Wetherby. Beyond Wetherby, the valley opens out and becomes part of the Vale of York.

Unlike other areas explored in this book, Wharfedale had no exploitable mineral deposits and, therefore, no canals to provide transport for them. Yorkshire's first worsted spinning mill was built in 1787 at Addingham, but by 1821, the village had taken up cotton manufacture with a population of 1,570. Similarly, the 1,200 population of Burley-in-Wharfedale worked in small cotton mills in the village. With these exceptions, the area was still predominantly agricultural. The distribution centre for corn to urban areas to the south was the market town of Otley and in 1831 it numbered over 3,000 inhabitants. Ilkley, by comparison, was a

The single-track Yorkshire Dales Railway ran north from Skipton and was opened in 1902 to Threshfield with connections to the Ilkley and Leeds line at Embsay Junction. The service was not a success and was withdrawn in 1930. However, freight traffic has been heavy and, even today, regular services of stone trains run from Swinden Quarry to Dewsbury, Hull, Leeds, Birmingham and Peterborough. In this photograph, from May 1968, BR Standard Class 4 4-6-0, 75019, slows for Rylstone level-crossing, where the crew will have to work the gates. JOHN HUNT small hamlet with less than 700. For these reasons the early railway schemes passed the valley by.

An Act of Parliament had been obtained jointly by the Lancashire and Yorkshire and North Eastern Railways (incorporated as the Wharfdale – note old spelling – Railway Company) in 1846 to build a line from Skipton through Ilkley and Otley to Arthington, but the scheme failed as the company could not raise the necessary capital and was wound up in 1852.

A second proposal was made in 1856 for a company called the Wharfedale Railway to construct a line on the same route as that authorized in 1846, but the promoters of this scheme could get no support from the major companies (the MR and the NER) who operated the lines into which the Wharfedale Railway would connect.

Finally, in 1860, following approaches from local representatives, the NER and the MR met and agreed to build a joint line between Otley and Ilkley. The MR would make a connection with the new line by building a branch from the L&BR at Apperley Bridge to a junction at Burley in Wharfedale and the NER would build a branch from its Leeds to Harrogate line at Arthington to make an end-on connection with the new line at Otley. The necessary Parliamentary powers were granted in 1861 with the passing of two acts: the Midland Railway (Otley and Ilkley Extension) Act 1861 and the North Eastern Railway (Extension to Otley and Ilkley) Act 1861.

Construction began in 1863 with the MR taking responsibility for building the line between Otley and Ilkley. The NER branch from Arthington was finished first, and the first train from Otley to Leeds, via Arthington, ran on 1 February 1865. The MR line from Apperley Junction, and the joint line itself, were completed a few months later and the first passenger train from Ilkley to Otley ran on 1 August 1865; freight services starting a year later, in October 1866.

To obtain its Act, the MR was required to provide no disadvantage to passengers to and from Bradford. This gave the Midland some problems as the journeys involved reversing trains at Apperley Junction. To alleviate this, the Midland sought powers to build a further line from Guiseley Junction (near Shipley) to Esholt Junction (near Guiseley). The line opened in December 1876 and the NER quickly negotiated running powers over the new section of line. This allowed the NER to run trains from Harrogate to Bradford without going via Leeds.

A final through connection to the joint line was made when the MR opened its Skipton–Ilkley line in 1888. The route was from the joint line at Ilkley and passed through Addingham, Bolton Abbey and Embsay, connecting with the Yorkshire Dales Railway Grassington branch at Embsay Junction, which it followed for the remaining mile or so to Skipton Station.

The route was closed as the result of the 'Beeching axe' in 1965 – passenger services were withdrawn on 22 March, whilst the remaining through goods services ended on 5 July. The route eventually closed to all traffic east of Embsay Junction in January 1966 (though access to the Haw Bank quarry sidings at Embsay Station survived until 1969) and was left to fall into disrepair. Around fourteen years after closure, a group of volunteers put forward a plan, in 1979, to reopen the line as a heritage railway. This plan was successful and Embsay railway station was refurbished throughout the second-half of the 1970s and reopened in 1981.

To the west of Embsay Station, a run-round loop for locomotives was built near the site of the former Embsay Junction, which had been disconnected when the line closed. By 1987, further extensions brought the line to a newly constructed halt at Holywell and later to Stoneacre Loop. Bolton Abbey railway station finally reopened in 1998, bringing the length of the heritage line to just over 4 miles (6.4km).

To operate the 1888 Skipton–Ilkley line, the two companies set up a joint committee, the Otley and Ilkley Joint Line Committee. In the early days, this led to some confusing arrangement, for example eastbound freight traffic for Leeds was sent on alternate weeks via Arthington and Apperley Junction to give fair distribution of income between the MR and the NER. Likewise, signalling was to be maintained in five-year periods, alternating between the two companies, an arrangement swiftly done away with and instead an agreement made that the Midland would signal west of Burley Junction, and the North Eastern the line east of Burley Junction.

As was to be expected, throughout its life most of the passenger traffic on the line was of a local nature and passengers seeking to travel further afield than Leeds, Bradford or Harrogate would need to change trains. North Eastern passenger services ran from Ilkley to Leeds via Otley, a slightly longer route than the Midland services, which ran via Apperley Junction – 18¾ miles (30.18km) via Otley compared to 16½ miles (26.55km) via Apperley Junction. By the time of the grouping, there were six trains each way on weekdays between Ilkley and Leeds, and eight trains running between Harrogate and Bradford. Midland services comprised eight trains each way between Leeds and Ilkley, and eleven trains between Ilkley and Bradford, with fifteen departures from Bradford to Ilkley, together with a limited number of trains between Otley and either Leeds or Bradford via Guiseley.

After the 1923 grouping, the line continued to be run on a joint basis by the LMSR and the LNER as the successors to the Midland and North Eastern companies. Weekday train services remained much the same and, by 1935, there were eight services each way on the LNER route. London, Midland and Scottish Railway services consisted of fourteen trains each way between Ilkley and Bradford (seven being through trains to/from Skipton) and nine between Ilkley and Leeds.

The Second World War had a dramatic effect on the line and even after the end of the war, services were poor compared to pre-war levels. In April 1946, LNER direct services between Ilkley and Leeds had fallen to just one, with a further six journeys possible by changing trains at Arthington. The Harrogate–Bradford service was reduced to two trains each way. London, Midland and Scottish Railway services were not much better, with seven trains Ilkley–Bradford and six Ilkley–Leeds.

With nationalization in 1948, there came an end to the joint committee and the entire line became part of the London Midland Region of British Railways, although this was short-lived and, in 1955, it became part of the North Eastern Region instead. Neither event had much effect on train services, and the 1957 timetable showed an improvement of services via Guiseley, but only four trains each way through Otley (all Ilkley–Leeds services) and the withdrawal of the Bradford–Harrogate service altogether.

A major change came in 1959 when passenger services over the line were moved from steam-hauled trains to DMU operation. The number of daily trains increased from forty-one to seventy-two, with hourly services Ilkley–Bradford and Ilkley–Leeds via Guiseley, although the Otley service remained at four services each way.

The increase in services had been welcomed, but only four years later the entire line was threatened. Under the Beeching proposals all the lines in Wharfedale would close along with the lines via Guiseley. However, due to pressures from the Ilkley Railway Supporters' Association (formed specially to fight the closure proposals), the Guiseley lines and the Burley–Ilkley section were reprieved. The line from Burley to Arthington was to close, along with the line north of Ilkley to Skipton. The last passenger services on the Burley–Arthington line ran on 20 March 1965 and goods services ceased on 5 July 1965. Ilkley became a terminus again with the withdrawal of the final freight services between Skipton and Ilkley in January 1966; the closed lines were demolished later that year.

The remaining lines were again threatened with closure in 1968, when a second closure proposal was made. The discussion went on until 1972, when it was announced that the Ilkley to Leeds service would survive but that the line between Guiseley and Shipley would close and once again trains between Ilkley and Bradford would have to reverse at Apperley Junction. The decision was, however, never implemented, as Bradford Corporation agreed to subsidize the line. Since 1974, the line has been managed by the West Yorkshire Passenger Transport Executive (WYPTE) – now branded West Yorkshire Metro – and is currently marketed as the Wharfedale line.

In common with the lines through Airedale and to Bradford, the Wharfedale line was electrified at 25kV AC overhead in 1994 and new British Rail Class 333 trains were introduced in the early 2000s. Investment in the line has seen passenger numbers grow, and now overcrowding on trains can be a problem at peak times.

CHAPTER 8

The Aire and Calder Watershed

Bulk transport in the valleys of the Aire and Calder before the railways was confined to the waterways and this proved to be a barrier to any town's commercial aspirations unless it had easy access to the navigable sections. The limitations of the hill-climbing abilities of early railway locomotives necessitated routes with gentle gradients. Thus, conventional wisdom dictated that towns, such as Bradford, Halifax, Batley, Cleckheaton and Wakefield could not reasonably expect to be connected by rail directly over the watershed. That they were, speaks volumes about the commercial risks taken by the railway company proprietors and the lengths to which their engineers had to go, developing railways in inhospitable territory. The major development pressure came from Bradford and it is worth taking a moment to see how the town developed, how the railway companies responded to the growing industrialization and how they left it ill prepared to counter competition from other major centres such as Leeds and Huddersfield.

In 1801, Bradford was a rural market town of 6,393 people, where wool-spinning and cloth-weaving were carried out in local cottages and farms. Bradford was, thus, not much bigger than nearby Keighley (5,745) and was significantly smaller than Halifax (8,866) and Huddersfield (7,268).

Industrialization began in the late eighteenth century when blast furnaces were established, in about 1788, by Hird, Dawson and Hardy at Low Moor and iron was worked by the Bowling Iron Company until about 1900. Yorkshire iron was used for shackles, hooks and piston rods for locomotives, colliery cages and other mining appliances where toughness was required. The Low Moor Company also made pig iron and employed 1,500 men in 1829. When the municipal borough of Bradford was created in 1847, there were forty-six coal mines within its boundaries. Coal output continued to expand, reaching a peak in 1868 when Bradford contributed a quarter of all the coal and iron produced in Yorkshire. The population of the township in 1841 was 34,560, a more than fivefold increase in forty years.

In 1825, the wool-combers' union called a strike that lasted for five months. They only returned to work because of the hardship they were suffering. Their absence from the mills led to the introduction of machine-combing, and more and more mechanization. The Industrial Revolution led to rapid growth, with wool imported in vast quantities for the manufacture of worsted cloth in which Bradford specialized, the town soon becoming known as the wool capital of the world.

Bradford had ample supplies of locally mined coal to provide the power that the industry needed. Local

BRADFORD ORIGINS

The name Bradford is derived from the Old English 'brad' and 'ford' meaning the broad ford. This is referring to a crossing of the Bradford Beck at Church Bank, around which a settlement grew in Saxon times. After an uprising in 1070 against William the Conqueror's 'Harrying of the North Campaign', the manor of Bradeford was laid waste and was recorded in the Domesday Book of 1086 as such.

It then became part of the Honour of Pontefract given to Ilbert de Lacy for services to the Conqueror, in whose family the manor remained until 1311. The manor then passed to the Earl of Lincoln, John of Gaunt, The Crown and, ultimately, private ownership in 1620.

By the Middle Ages, Bradford had become a small town centred on Kirkgate, Westgate and Ivegate. As early as 1316, there is mention of a fulling mill, a soke mill (where all the manors' corn was milled) and a market. Edward IV granted the right to hold two annual fairs and from this time the town began to prosper. In the reign of Henry VIII, Bradford exceeded Leeds as a manufacturing centre. Bradford grew slowly over the next 200 years as the woollen trade gained in prominence.

During the Civil War, the town was garrisoned for the Parliamentarians and, in 1642, was unsuccessfully attacked by Royalist forces from Leeds. Sir Thomas Fairfax took the command of the garrison and marched his soldiers and new recruits to his headquarters at Tadcaster. This left Bradford woefully undefended and the Earl of Newcastle, in charge of the Royalist army that had already captured much of the West Riding, seized the opportunity. Setting up headquarters at Bolling Hall, the Royalists besieged the town resulting in its surrender. The Civil War caused a decline in industry but after the accession of William III and Mary II, in 1689, prosperity began to return. The launch of manufacturing in the early eighteenth century marked the start of the town's development, while new canal and turnpike road links encouraged trade.

---

sandstone was an excellent resource for building the mills and, with a population of 182,000 by 1850 (another fivefold increase in only nine years), the town grew rapidly as workers were attracted by jobs in the textile mills. A desperate shortage of water in Bradford Dale was a serious limitation to industrial expansion and improvement in urban sanitary conditions. In 1854, Bradford Corporation bought the Bradford Water Company and embarked on a huge engineering programme to bring supplies of soft water from Airedale, Wharfedale and Nidderdale. Thus, by 1882, the water supply and quality had radically improved. Meanwhile, urban expansion took place along the routes out of the city toward the Hortons and Bowling, and the townships became part of a continuous urban area by the late nineteenth century.

Bradford's eighteenth century pre-eminence in the wool trade was beginning to be hampered by the cost of transport – the town is not on a river of any size and is in a deep valley. During the 1760s and 1770s, a group of Bradford businessmen were the driving force behind the creation of the West Riding end of the Leeds and Liverpool Canal (L&L Canal) and its offshoot the Bradford Canal, with a view to facilitating easy and reliable transport to and from the town.

The Bradford Canal was a 4-mile (6.4km) spur from the L&L Canal at Shipley. It was built to connect Bradford with the Skipton limestone quarries, the industrial towns on both sides of the Pennines and the ports of Liverpool and Goole. It opened in 1774 but had something of a chequered life.

Initially, the main cargo was stone, with several kilns built beside the canal by the Bradford Lime Kiln Company, the limestone being brought from Skipton. Coal-pit owners on the south side of Bradford, in Broomfields and Bowling, built tramways into the town but there was no direct connection with the canal, as possible routes were blocked by buildings. In about 1790, the newly established Bowling Ironworks constructed a wagonway from its works in Bowling to a staithe at Golden Lyon Yard about 200yd (180m) south of the canal basin. Finished iron products and coal were exported from the town by the canal via the wagonway. The carriage of wool from Australia was an important source of revenue from the 1820s, and from 1828, packet boats carried passengers to Selby and Leeds. However, the canal was beset by difficulties.

With no means to transport their stone, several merchants started to negotiate with the Leeds and Liverpool, the Aire and Calder, and Bradford Council to take over the remains of the canal. These negotiations were successful and a new company,

BRADFORD CANAL WATER-SUPPLY ISSUES

Water supply is a significant issue for any canal company and this company was no exception. As Bradford grew, the canal basin was surrounded by housing, with pollution from sewage occurring. Further down, mills drew water from the canal, used it for industrial processes and then returned it to the canal in polluted form. The Company had bought up tracts of land, at the end of the eighteenth century, to obtain water rights, and had dammed the Bradford Beck, even though their authorizing Act of Parliament had specifically excluded it as a source of water. The Bradford Board of Surveyors commented on the filth and stench in a report made in 1844, and an outbreak of cholera five years later, in which 406 people died, prompted the city council to act. A wide-ranging sanitation bill was prepared, which included a clause to buy the canal and close it. The action would be funded by a £100,000 public loan. The bill went before Parliament, but concerted opposition by the Leeds and Liverpool Canal, the Aire and Calder Navigation, the Bradford Canal Company and other industrialists, succeeded in reducing the amount of the loan to £50,000, which was insufficient to enable the canal to be purchased.

Hot weather in 1864 led to a fund being opened so that a court order could be used to close the canal on the basis that it was a public nuisance. A local newspaper, *The Bradford Observer*, described it as 'that seething cauldron of all impurity, the Bradford Canal'. Although the Company argued that the water was polluted before it entered the canal, a successful injunction was granted on 6 November 1866 preventing them from taking water from the Bradford Beck. An offer by the Leeds and Liverpool Canal to take it over and clean it up was rejected by those who had sought the injunction. Closure was postponed until 1 May 1867, while both the Bradford Company and the Leeds and Liverpool attempted to obtain an Act of Parliament, but both failed, leading to the canal being closed and drained.

the Bradford Canal Company Limited, was formed and bought most of the canal from the old company for £2,500. The section above Northbrook Bridge was sold to developers and, on 21 March 1870, the old company was wound up. The new company expected to get a water supply from two reservoirs and three streams, and hoped to supplement this with a pipeline running from the top of the Leeds and Liverpool's Bingley locks. This suggestion was not acceptable to the Leeds and Liverpool, so the new company had to resort to building steam-pumping engines at each lock to pump water back up the canal. The section from Shipley to Oliver Lock was reopened in 1872, five years to the day since it had closed, and the top section was reopened the following April. Although the stone traffic, which had been around 125,000 tons (113,400 tonnes) per year prior to closure, returned, most of the other traffic had moved to the railway and did not. The canal finally closed and was abandoned in 1922.

Despite this, the canals were very successful for Bradford but, from the 1830s, successors to the eighteenth-century businessmen were impressed by the new railways being built around the country and, again, Bradford businessmen were in the vanguard of proposals to enable the town to benefit from this new and exciting form of transport. Various schemes were started, but none received enough support. An approach was made to the North Midland Railway to try and persuade the company to extend its Derby to Leeds line to the town. Unfortunately, the appeal fell on deaf ears.

In 1840, the Manchester and Leeds line opened between Hebden Bridge and Normanton, and at Brighouse was tantalizingly close to Bradford at only 6½ miles (10.4km). A coach service was started to connect with the trains at Brighouse, taking an hour to buck and sway over the indifferent roads. Despite the rigours of the journey, 40,000 passengers were carried in 1844. Hopes that something better might be proposed were dashed when the Manchester & Leeds Railway (M&LR) announced that it had no intention of extending the North Dean to Halifax branch to the wool capital. (North Dean was renamed Greetland in 1897.)

Whilst the M&LR was, clearly, dismissive of the transport needs of the Bradford merchants, these same merchants succeeded in going it alone and forming a new company, the Leeds and Bradford Railway (L&BR), in 1843 with George Hudson as chairman. Hudson was also chairman of the North Midland and, in 1844, he had persuaded the NMR and two other companies he controlled to merge, forming the Midland Railway. The L&BR obtained the necessary Act of Parliament in July of 1843, to build a line from Wellington Street, Leeds, to Brad-

Tackling the steady climb on the L&YR Calder Valley line toward Summit Tunnel on 3 May 1968, is LMS Class 8F 2-8-0, 48321, with a coal train. Due to be withdrawn from service just over a month after the date of this picture, the 8F was a native of Newton Heath shed. JOHN HUNT

ford via Shipley and a link to the North Midland's terminus at Hunslet Lane, to allow connections to the south.

They appointed George Stephenson to survey the route and engineer the line. He routed the line up the Aire Valley to Shipley, and then turned south and followed Bradford Dale to Bradford – the only reasonably flat approach to the town.

The M&LR Company's apparent lack of interest in serving Bradford from the Halifax direction led to the newly formed Leeds and Bradford Railway seeing a commercial opportunity and promised to construct the line. For some reason, the M&LR took exception to this and applied for powers to construct a line from Mirfield through the Spen Valley, descending into Bradford on rope-worked inclines as steep as 1 in 25, considering tunnels to be 'difficult and dangerous'. Fortunately, this was successfully opposed by both the L&BR and the Leeds, Dewsbury and Manchester Railway.

To get support for its Act of incorporation, the L&BR had made promises to build several 'extension' lines. These became commitments once the Act was approved and, therefore, much as they might wish to, could not be ignored. To carry out these obligations, the L&BR formed the West Yorkshire Railway to build lines from the L&BR Bradford terminus to Sowerby Bridge via Halifax; Low Moor to Mirfield and Dewsbury; and from Low Moor to a junction with the L&BR and another with the Leeds, Dewsbury and Manchester Railway at Wortley. The M&LR, conscious of being edged out of Bradford in much the same way as it had in Leeds, retaliated by promoting a separate scheme, the Leeds and West Riding Junction Railway. This proposal closely followed the route of the L&BR scheme but utilized atmospheric propulsion on the inclines each side of the summit. Both lines were considered in the 1845 session of Parliament and both were rejected.

The M&LR was still keen to get access to a route to Leeds via Bradford that did not involve running powers over the North Midland route from Normanton to Leeds. With this in mind, it proposed a merger with the L&BR and, much to everyone's surprise, the L&BR chairman, George Hudson, agreed. In view of this development, George Stephenson suggested that the two competing proposals should be combined. This was agreed and the new railway was to be called the West Riding Union Railway. It would have its own station in Bradford but the L&BR would build a cross-town link between the two systems. Unfortunately, in July 1846, the L&BR withdrew from the proposed merger following the M&LR altering clauses in the agreement to the detriment of the other party and immediately offered to lease itself to the Midland Railway. George Hudson was, of course, chairman of both companies and, rather surprisingly, chaired the meeting at which the lease was agreed. He proposed a payment to the L&BR that was considered very favourable at the time and brought much criticism when he fell from grace. The L&BR was merged with the Midland in 1851. Needless to say, the proposed link from its Bradford Station to the new West Riding Union Railway Station was abandoned.

This spat between the two companies was to have profound consequences for Bradford. It left a permanent legacy of two separate termini only 300yd (273m) apart and prevented the city being on a through railway route. Many consider this resulted in Bradford being something of a poor neighbour to Leeds.

The West Riding Union Railway Act of 18 August 1846 authorized a line supported by the Manchester and Leeds Railway; the Act required amalgamation with that company within three months. This was done on 17 November, but the compulsory nature of the merger did not find much favour in Yorkshire. The Manchester Company was the subject of much criticism, mostly about the shocking services it provided, but tinged with some of the old county rivalry and a general feeling that a railway with its roots in the cotton industry couldn't possibly understand the woollen trade! To antagonize the Yorkshire interests still further, the company had to apply to the Board of Trade for a two-year extension to build its line.

East of Mirfield, on 3 May 1968, a loaded coal train passes the remains of the junction with the Spen Valley line. It is hauled by ex-LMS 8F 2-8-0, 48321, of Newton Heath depot, working out its final days before BR dispensed with steam traction for good.
JOHN HUNT

Ex-LNER type B1 4-6-0 'at home' on Low Moor shed in the summer of 1966. It is standing over the ash pit ready for disposal. Low Moor had as many as fifty locomotives allocated in the 1950s but, by the time of this photograph, this had been reduced to seventeen.
JOHN HUNT

Crossing the L&YR Bowling Junction from the Bradford direction is LMS Black Five 4-6-0, 44693, on 27 May 1967, two days before withdrawal from traffic. The line coming in from the right, from Laisterdyke, is the erstwhile Leeds, Bradford and Halifax Junction Railway, later to become part of the GNR.
JOHN HUNT

Railways around Bradford 1884.

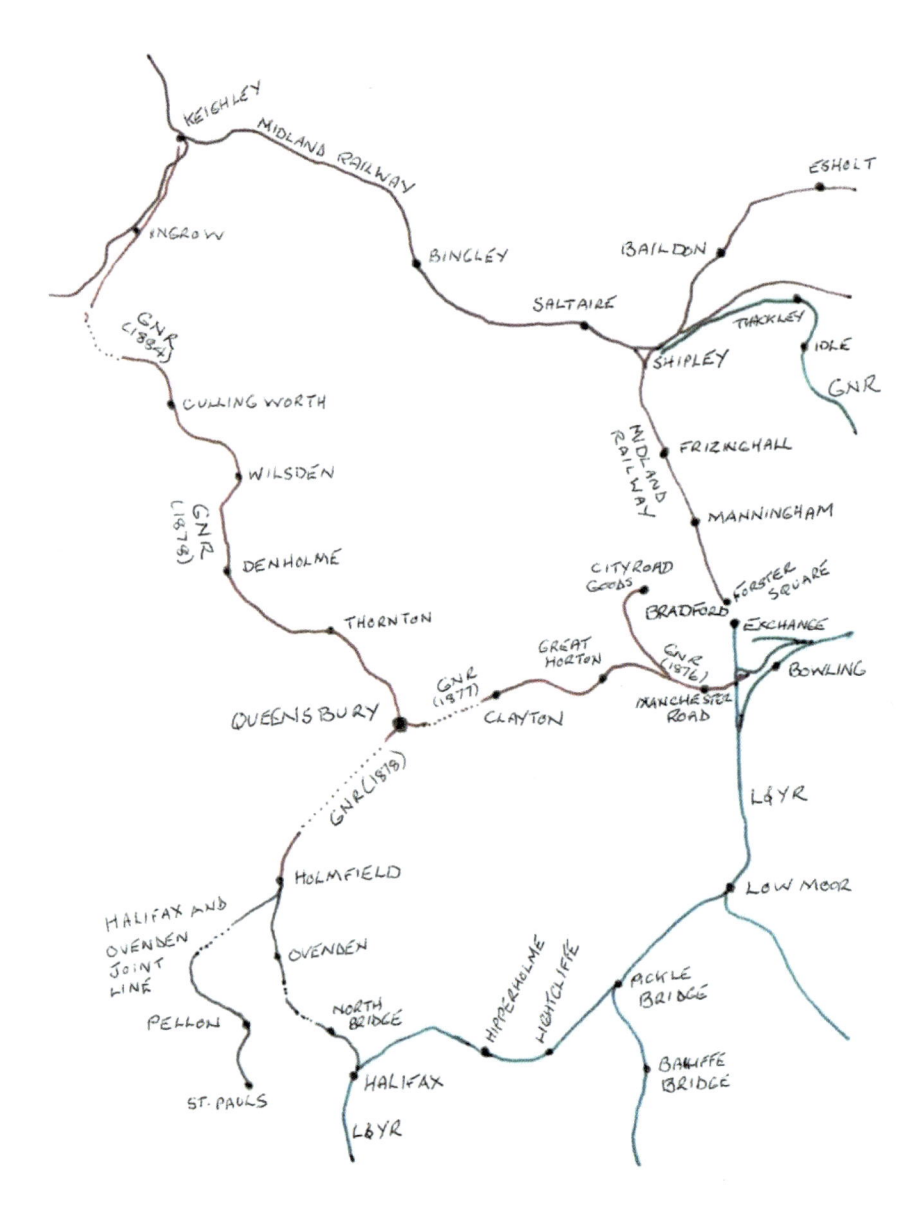

The actual construction of the line was carried out by the M&LR, which merged with four other railway companies the following year to become the Lancashire and Yorkshire Railway (L&YR). The section from Low Moor to Mirfield (the Spen Valley line) was opened on 18 July 1848, but the more difficult construction from Bradford to Low Moor was delayed until 9 May 1850 and Mirfield to Halifax to 7 August 1850.

With the arrival in Bradford of the L&YR in May 1850, the existing Leeds and Bradford Station received 'Midland' as a suffix to its name and became known as Forster Square in 1924. The L&YR line from Low Moor terminated at a new station in Drake Street. This was constructed jointly by the L&YR and GNR and became known as Bradford Exchange.

When the Leeds, Bradford and Halifax Junction Railway (later absorbed by the Great Northern) arrived in Bradford, it initially built a terminus at Adolphus Street. Despite being an imposing structure architecturally, it was considered to be too far out of the town centre and this led the railways' proprietors, the GNR, to decide to build an extension to Exchange Station in which it already had part ownership. A branch line was built from east of the Adolphus Street terminus that looped south and joined the existing L&YR line at Mill Lane Junction. With this new access in place, Adolphus Street Station was closed to passenger traffic in 1867, but remained in use for parcels and freight traffic until 1972. The station was demolished shortly after and is now the home of the Bradford fruit and vegetable market.

Bradford Exchange Station was completely rebuilt on the same site in 1880 with ten bay platforms and two arched roofs. Constructed of wrought iron, these rested at the outer sides on plain stone walls with classical Corinthian-style columns down the middle. Glass covered the middle half and timber (inside) plus slate (outside) covered the outer quarters of each span. The four end screens were glazed in a fan pattern with decorative timber outer edging. The train shed was 450ft (140m) long, 100ft (30m) wide for each arch with a height of 80ft (24m) from track to apex. Surprisingly, the station never had a formal frontage; instead, passengers entered rather apologetically by an opening in the north-west side.

In its 1920s heyday, routes served included Wakefield Westgate via Ardsley (used by many of the city's through trains to London, King's Cross), Wakefield, Kirkgate via Batley and Ossett, Keighley and Halifax via Queensbury, Mirfield via Cleckheaton (the Spen Valley line) and to Leeds via the Pudsey Loop, in addition to the current lines. These, however, had all closed by the end of 1966 – most having fallen victim to the 'Beeching axe'.

By 1973, the railway station with its ten platforms was deemed too large and was again rebuilt, this time on a different site slightly further south. The old Exchange Station was demolished soon afterwards and was used for a time as a car park; the site now houses Bradford Crown Court. In 1977, a bus station was built alongside and, in 1983, the station was renamed Bradford Interchange to link buses and trains in a covered environment.

The bus station featured a large ridge-and-furrow design of overall roof, which didn't last long and was

Making an impressive departure from Bradford Exchange Station, in early September 1967, is LNER-designed B1 4-6-0, 61306, with a train for Leeds. Note the overall glazed roof of the soon-to-be-demolished station. JOHN HUNT

LMS Stanier 2-6-4T, 42616, makes a spirited exit from Bradford Exchange for Leeds on 2 September 1967. JOHN HUNT

BELOW: *Two ex-LMS Stanier Black Fives (44694 and 44662) emerge side by side from Bradford Exchange Station on 26 August 1967. Both were locally based at Low Moor shed and both were withdrawn in little over a month after this image was captured.* JOHN HUNT

THE SOUND OF BUFFERS

Buffers and trains have been firm bedfellows since the earliest days of railways. But in the twenty-first century, we no longer hear the clank and scream of buffers coming together as we once did.

Older readers will be able to cast their minds back to childhood and perhaps recall the sound of a long, loose-coupled coal train as it starts to brake when going downhill. Only a minor clanging as the first few wagons come together but a rapidly increasing crescendo of noise as the wagons close up culminating in a might crash as the last few make contact. As a child, the author used to listen to the nocturnal shunting activities when staying at my grandparents' house just off Chanterlands Avenue in Hull, the action stemming from the Ideal Standard radiator factory on National Avenue. The noise reached such deafening heights that, using all of my youthful 'experience' and 'knowledge', I would firmly declare that that last particularly loud bang must have been a derailment. Fortunately, my grandfather, a career railwayman, was able to use his experience and knowledge and accurately define the normality of what we had heard.

At Low Moor shed, a study in black and white over the buffer beams in 1965. JOHN HUNT

---

demolished in 1999 to allow for a rebuilding of the bus station, which was opened in 2001. During the 1970s and 1980s, the Exchange Station was considered the principal station for Bradford with express services to London King's Cross, trans-Pennine services to Liverpool and Newcastle, and summer Saturday services to the south-west. The intercity services were moved to Forster Square Station in 1992 when the line to Leeds and Skipton was electrified. Like most mainline stations, a Red Star Parcels' facility was available. Unfortunately, the privatization of British Rail resulted in it losing this during the 1990s.

There is no doubt that having two important railway stations in one city is not conducive to sensible development of services and facilities. Over the years, as already noted, Bradford has probably lost out to Leeds because of this.

There have been many schemes to provide a link between Bradford's two railway terminals. The major redevelopment of the city centre in the 1960s provided an opportunity to connect the termini but was not pursued. This was a time when the car was 'king' and decision-makers could not be persuaded of the strategic importance of such a link. The hilly nature of the city provides the biggest challenge, as one station is much further up the hill than the other: Bradford Interchange is at the end of a long slope, steep by railway standards, but is many feet higher than Forster Square. This gradient is not unprecedented in railway construction and the relocation of Forster Square further from the city centre has provided additional space in which the transition could be accomplished; unfortunately, large buildings were constructed on the alignment in the 1990s.

In 1850, with the opening of the Spen Valley line between Bradford and Low Moor, it was possible to reach Wakefield from Bradford. The journey was not usually a satisfying experience because of the long wait for a connection at Mirfield. A more direct route was proposed by the Leeds, Bradford and Halifax Junction Railway (LB&HJR) with a branch to Gildersome. The proposal was essentially a line

Bradford's original station was the Midland Railway's Forster Square site. The principal locomotive shed for the Midland and LMS was Manningham, a little way down the line toward Shipley. Opened in 1872, it was a substantial 'roundhouse' structure with an allocation of about forty locomotives. However, by the time of this picture (early 1966), closure was looming and the allocation was about fourteen. The B1, 61121, was a visitor from Doncaster and was withdrawn from that depot soon after this picture was taken. JOHN HUNT

BR Standard Class 5, 4-6-0, 73053, is seen near Batley in August 1967. The loco is a bit of a 'foreigner' in the West Riding, being based at Patricroft in Manchester. JOHN HUNT

for the coal traffic, but it soon became apparent that by extending to Ardsley, a more direct route from Bradford to Wakefield could be achieved. The Gildersome branch was authorized by Parliament in 1853, with the extension to Ardsley following on 10 July 1854. The branch was completed and opened in 1856 and was soon conveying about 1,000 tons (907 tonnes) of coal a day to Bradford. The extension was completed and opened on 10 October 1857, with through Bradford expresses from King's Cross using the line from 1 December.

During the late nineteenth century, Batley was the centre of the shoddy and mungo trade, in which wool rags and clothes were recycled by reweaving them into blankets, carpets and uniforms. In 1861 there were at least thirty shoddy mills in Batley. The owners of these recycling businesses were known as the 'shoddy barons'. There was a 'shoddy king' and a 'shoddy temple', properly known as the Zion Chapel. The first railway to reach Batley was the London and North Western in 1848, and the GNR-backed Leeds, Bradford and Halifax Junction Railway (LB&HJR) arrived in November 1864, with a branch line from Adwalton Junction on the Gildersome line.

The Queensbury Lines

At the beginning of this chapter, reference was made to the difficulties of constructing railways over the watershed itself. West of the Spen Valley and Bradford Dale, the ridge rapidly rises to over 1,000ft (305m) and broadens into a plateau broken by steep-sided valleys. Despite the difficulties of engineering routes through these physical features, promotors of new lines were plentiful, but not always successful. There were several attempts to shorten the Aire Valley route between Bradford and Colne, towns with much stronger trading links than today. Proposals in 1857 and 1866 were both rejected by Parliament. Attention then turned to linking Halifax and Bradford with Keighley. Crossing the difficult terrain was expensive and all the lines over the ridge of the watershed were marked by a number of major civil engineering works that included several viaducts and tunnels.

A feature of the line was the unusual station at Queensbury, which had a triangular track layout, with two platforms on each of the three chords. As all of the lines eventually constructed passed through Queensbury, the group became known as the Queensbury lines. All the lines were either solely owned by the GNR or jointly by the GNR and the L&YR. The lines were:

- The Halifax and Ovenden Junction Railway, opened from 1874.
- The Bradford and Thornton Railway, opened in stages from 1876.
- The Halifax, Thornton and Keighley Railway from Holmfield to Queensbury and from Thornton to Keighley, opened in stages from 1878.
- The Halifax High Level Railway, opened from 1890, but closed to passengers in 1917.

The town of Halifax is very hilly and the first railway station, opened on 1 July 1844, was at Shaw Syke and was the terminus of a branch line from the M&LR's line to Normanton. With the opening of the line between Halifax and Bradford, on 7 August 1850, a new station was opened about 220yd (200m) east of the original. This new station had temporary wooden buildings pending the construction of a permanent structure, which was completed and opened on 23 June 1855.

The station is approached from the north-east by a tunnel and is located at the bottom of the town. From 1854, the GNR had running powers to Halifax over the LB&HJR. Both the L&YR and the GNR were concerned about the difficulty of carting goods to and from the higher lying districts, as well as congestion at the station itself. The Ovenden Valley, north-west of the town, was the source of considerable volumes of traffic, all of which had to be carted from Halifax Station. The provision of a branch line through the valley was a logical step and would, potentially, reduce the congestion in the main station.

Almost by coincidence, a company was formed, in 1863, to build a railway between Halifax and Keighley along the Thornton Valley north-west of Queensbury. At the time this was considered

Hammering away from Bradford Exchange toward St Dunstans on the GNR line to Leeds, is LMS Fairburn Class 4, 2-6-4T, 42251. Based at Low Moor shed for the last few months of its working life in 1967, 42251 was withdrawn in October of that year. JOHN HUNT

to be a very ambitious project and during its time in Parliament, the scheme was much reduced to merely connect Halifax with Holmfield through the Ovenden Valley. The revised scheme was titled the Halifax and Ovenden Junction Railway and it was incorporated on 30 June 1864. The GNR and L&YR each subscribed a third of the capital and agreed to work the line jointly.

The new company struggled to raise the remainder of the capital that it needed, resulting in construction of the line being much delayed. A further Act of 12 August 1867 was obtained, permitting a doubling of the authorized capital, some deviations of the route and an extension of time. Nevertheless, the depressed state of the money market meant that the scheme lay dormant until a further Act was obtained on 1 August 1870, sanctioning a second extension of time and vesting the undertaking jointly in the GNR and L&YR. The concern was then renamed the Halifax and Ovenden Joint Railway. Soon afterwards, construction began from a junction with the L&YR at the north end of Halifax Station, for 2 miles 48 chains (4.2km) to Holmfield. The engineering was fearsome, with gradients as steep as 1 in 45 and the sharpest curve was 11 chains radius (0.24km). A substantial masonry viaduct carried the line through Halifax, with thirty-five spans, which varied from 35 to 44ft (10.5–13m). A short distance beyond that, the line crossed another viaduct of eleven spans, which varied from 20 to 35ft (6–10.5m). There were two tunnels: North Bridge (403yd/363m) and Lee Bank (267yd/240m)). Earthworks were heavy, with high retaining walls.

Goods depots were opened at North Bridge and Holmfield. The line opened for goods between Halifax and North Bridge on 17 August 1874, to Holmfield on 1 September 1874 and was opened to passengers throughout on 1 December 1879.

Bradford and Thornton Railway

Turning now to the Bradford and Thornton Railway. Thornton was an important industrial centre and, in 1865, separate proposals were advanced by the L&YR and the GNR for lines to Thornton, but they were rejected by Parliament. During 1870, local businessmen put forward a scheme for a railway from Bradford to Thornton via Clayton and Queensbury to reach industrial locations hitherto not served by railways. Motivated by a strong desire to keep the Midland Railway out, the GNR agreed to sponsor the scheme and subscribe half the capital. The GNR felt that unless it got in first, the MR would step in and get access to Halifax. Accordingly, the Bradford and Thornton Railway Act was passed on 24 July 1871, sponsored by the GNR, and the undertaking was transferred to, and vested in, the GNR by an Act of 18 July 1872. The authorized construction was 5 miles 49 chains (9km) of line between St Dunstans (Bradford) and Thornton. In addition, there was to be a short branch to Brick Lane, on the west side of Bradford, where a goods station was to be established, to be called City Road.

A major objective of the Bradford and Thornton Railway was to provide railway facilities for Queensbury, home of the important Black Dyke Mills, run by a textile manufacturer, John Foster. The town was easily the most important on the route but, unfortunately, the town was at an altitude of 1,150ft (345m) above sea level, making it well-nigh impossible for the railway to get close to it. The result was that the distance from the town to the station was 1 mile (1.6km) downhill along an unmade and unlit footpath, with a difference in altitude of about 400ft (120m). When the line opened in 1878, there was no station at Queensbury until a temporary structure was hastily made ready for Easter 1879; it was located east of the East Junction. It had no goods facilities, no access for vehicles and, as already noted, the only footpath was unmade and unlit. There was repeated pressure from the Queensbury Local Board to improve the access, but the GNR dissembled. In 1885, it considered a report, which showed that it would be possible to construct a new station with platforms on all three sides of the triangular junction. Remarkably, a railway connection to the town was considered: either a rope-worked incline at a gradient of 1 in 6, or a slightly more conventional locomotive-worked line, following a roundabout route. The latter would cost twice as much: it would be 2 miles (3.2km) in length with a maximum gradient of 1 in 30. Work started on the new station in 1889 and a road to the town was included in the plans. The station opened on 1 January 1890 and the road came into use soon afterwards. The railway connection schemes were quietly forgotten.

The weaving industry had flourished in this inhospitable location because of coal supplies in the immediate area. Originally, the coal supplies were plentiful but there were now fears that the deposits were nearing the end of their life, so the presence of the GNR line assured future supplies.

Construction of the Bradford and Thornton Railway started on 21 March 1874. The earthworks were heavy, and construction was slow. The first section to be opened was from the St Dunstan's junctions at Bradford, as far as Great Horton on 4 December 1876. The short branch line to City Road goods depot opened on the same day; both openings were for goods traffic only. The short extension to Clayton followed by 9 August 1877. The next stage was dependent on completion of Clayton Tunnel and Thornton Viaduct. Over a year was to pass before the line was opened throughout to all traffic on 14 October 1878. Thornton Viaduct was typical of the substantial civil engineering that this area demands. Crossing the Pinch Beck Valley, the viaduct is 300yd (270m) long and rises 120ft (36m) from the valley floor. It was built of brick and stone quarried locally and the central piers were sunk

25ft (7.5m) underground to the foundations. Each of its twenty arches is of 40ft (12m) span. It is still (in 2020) standing.

The triangular station layout at Queensbury was almost unique in the UK (the only other one being at Ambergate on the Midland Railway). There were three signal boxes at the station, one for each junction on the three station approaches from Bradford, Keighley and Halifax. After the 1879 opening, the station remained in full use for seventy-six years, closing to passengers in 1955 and completely in 1963. Almost all the station infrastructure has now been demolished.

Next to be developed was the Halifax, Thornton and Keighley Railway from Holmfield to Queensbury and from Thornton to Keighley. In 1864, and again in 1867, moves had been made independently (although seeking help from the Midland Railway) for a rail link between Huddersfield, Halifax and Keighley, but these were unsuccessful. The promoters tried again in 1872 but the Midland Railway was not interested and refused to assist. The GNR was also 'lukewarm' to the promoters at first, preferring to pursue their own scheme. However, on 23 December 1872, agreement with the independent promoters was reached. The GNR would not support their line from Halifax to Huddersfield but undertook to adopt the proposal for a shorter railway between Halifax and Keighley, if the independent supporters would find half the cost. The GNR's financial commitment was £640,000.

The Great Northern Railway (Halifax, Thornton & Keighley Railway) Act was passed on 5 August 1873. The route was to start from the almost-completed Halifax and Ovenden line at Holmfield, and join with the Bradford and Thornton Railway at Queensbury. It would then extend the line from Thornton on to Keighley.

Between Holmfield and Queensbury the 2¼ mile (3.6km) line was almost entirely within Queensbury Tunnel or the massive Strines Cutting. Considerable trouble was encountered with water-bearing strata during construction. The same problem was encountered with the 1,033yd (940m) long and 59ft (18.2m) deep cutting, with even greater difficulties than in the tunnel with the water-bearing strata, holding up the opening of this section to passengers until 1 December 1879, although goods trains started running on 14 October 1878.

In 1878, the GNR was in serious financial difficulty on capital account and invited the Midland Railway to join in the Keighley line works. Not unsurprisingly, the Midland refused!

Passenger trains began to run from Bradford to Halifax on 1 December 1879. Initially, they ran non-stop after Queensbury, but a temporary station was provided at Holmfield within a fortnight. North Bridge Station opened on 25 March 1880 and Ovenden Station in June 1881. The Halifax to Holmfield section remained in joint ownership with the L&YR. Both companies ran goods trains but the GNR alone provided the passenger service. Queensbury was not reached from Ovenden until late 1879, the line opening for goods traffic on 1 December and to passenger services two weeks later when temporary platforms at Holmfield were brought into use. Two temporary platforms at Queensbury had been in use for several months for Bradford–Thornton trains and completion of the long-awaited Halifax route gave the station a great deal of importance because of its junction status. Initially, a daily service of six trains each way was provided between Bradford and Halifax.

Contractors started boring the 1 mile 741yd (2.28km) Queensbury tunnel on 21 May 1874. This was to be the longest tunnel on the GNR until the opening of Ponsbourne Tunnel, near Hertford, in 1910. Four streets of temporary houses were built in Queensbury for the construction workers and were named, rather unimaginatively, Oakley, Great, Northern and Railway Streets! Although supposedly temporary, the buildings were not condemned until 1957. The tunnel work was completed on 31 July 1878.

Work on the £282,000 Thornton to Keighley section proved to be exceptionally difficult and progress was slow. The most serious problems were encountered on the stretch between Denholme and Wilsden, where repeated landslips frustrated progress with construction. The intention had been for the line to pass through a series of cuttings, but the persistence of these earth slips forced the GNR to substitute two short tunnels.

In 1880, the GNR applied for Parliamentary sanction to reduce its financial liability for the Thornton to Keighley line on which work was about to begin. It approached the Midland Railway with a proposal to make a joint station at Keighley, to be used by the Midland Railway main-line trains, the Worth Valley line trains and the GNR. Surprisingly, the Midland Railway were amenable to this and, by an agreement of 1 June 1881, the Midland granted the GNR the necessary running powers and agreed to make a new junction station. The agreement was in exchange for the Midland getting certain traffic concessions to Halifax.

Goods trains began running from Thornton to Denholme on a single-track alignment from September 1882. Passenger operation to Denholme started on 1 January 1884. The line was opened to Keighley goods' depot on 1 April 1884, but the joint passenger station at Keighley was not ready. From 7 April 1884, GNR passenger trains were extended to Ingrow with eight trains a day. Finally, on 1 November 1884, passenger trains began running from Bradford and Halifax to Keighley Joint Station. There were eighteen GNR trains each weekday and four on Sundays. The station had cost £80,000 and, in fact, was not completed until the following spring.

The northernmost part of the Worth Valley branch was relaid and doubled; the agreement marked the start of a more amicable relationship between the GNR and the Midland. Powers for the new Keighley Station and for the widening of the last part of the Worth Valley line were granted by an Act of 1882. Although agreement had been reached about a shared passenger station, goods facilities at Keighley were kept entirely separate: the GNR built a spur line off the Worth Valley route just outside Keighley Station; the spur crossed under and entered its own goods yard.

There were some impressive engineering features on the Thornton to Keighley section, with massive viaducts at Thornton, Hewenden and Cullingworth. Denholme Station, 850ft (263m) above sea level, served another elevated woollen township, preceded by a descent averaging 1 in 50 for 5 miles (8km). Lees Moor Tunnel on the route to Bradford continued the trying conditions, turning through more than 90 degrees in its 1,533yd (1.39km) length.

Queensbury Station operated as an interchange point, making useful local connections. At certain times of the day, trains stood on all three sides of the triangle, allowing connections to be made in all directions. In 1910, there were twenty-two weekday departures from Bradford Exchange to Halifax or Keighley. In most cases, the destination not served by a direct train could be reached by changing at Queensbury. There were twenty-one trains from Halifax for the Queensbury line and sixteen starting from Keighley. On Sundays, nine trains left Bradford Exchange for Halifax or Keighley. The journey from Bradford to Halifax by this route took between 35 and 40 minutes depending on the number of stops and the duration of the wait at Queensbury. This was slower than by the alternative Lancashire and Yorkshire Railway service, which was also more frequent. A Great Northern train from Bradford to Keighley took 45 minutes, twice as long as the faster trains by the Midland Railway from Forster Square.

Some traffic was lost to the electric tramways after the turn of the century. The Bradford trams began to eat into the traffic at stations as far as Thornton, whilst Ovenden, Holmfield and Queensbury became prey to the Halifax tramways. Because of the breaks of gauge, trams were not a threat on longer journeys in the West Riding, but when buses were operating in later years, their threat was considerable.

The Queensbury lines cost close on £1m to build and many commentators have doubted that the traffic ever justified spending so large a sum. After dallying with through expresses to London, the lines settled down to meeting the need for more local services. For some time, the network was busy, both for passengers and goods, but carryings declined steeply after the introduction of the all-conquering bus after the First World War abstracted much traffic. Passenger services were discontinued in 1955 and goods traffic ceased in 1974.

CHAPTER 9

The Calder Valley

The River Calder rises on Heald Moor in Lancashire and then flows east into West Yorkshire through green countryside, former woollen-mill villages, and large and small towns before joining the River Aire near Castleford. The river's valley is generally known as the Calder Valley. In transportation terms the valley is regarded as one of the key trans-Pennine crossing routes because at no point does it rise to more than 600ft (180m) above sea level. It flows for a distance of around 45 miles (72km) through Todmorden, Hebden Bridge, Mytholmroyd, Luddendenfoot, Sowerby Bridge, Elland, Brighouse, Mirfield, Dewsbury, Horbury Bridge and on to Wakefield. The river does not flow through the centres of Halifax and Huddersfield, which are on the Calder's main tributaries, Hebble Brook and the River Colne, respectively. The only large town centres through which the Calder flows are Brighouse, Mirfield, Dewsbury and the city of Wakefield. The river itself is only navigable in short sections, but these sections are connected by artificial 'cuts' (for example Horbury Cut) to form the Calder and Hebble Navigation, an important transport link in the eighteenth century.

The river was key to the success of the textile industries and flows through an area known as the Yorkshire Heavy Woollen District. Many major mills were constructed along its banks, particularly at Dewsbury and Wakefield. These developments were not confined to the larger towns, with the smaller communities of Hebden Bridge, Sowerby Bridge and Todmorden, as well as along the tributaries, the Hebble at Halifax and the Colne at Huddersfield, all seeing significant activity. The mills in the Upper Calder Valley specialized in cotton-weaving, with some cotton-spinning, whilst those in the lower part of the valley specialized in wool and shoddy.

The river formed an important transportation system for raw materials and the products of the mills, particularly prior to the development of other infrastructures, such as canal and railway links to the area.

The race to construct a long-distance trans-Pennine canal to connect the port of Liverpool with the woollen districts of the West Riding, as we observed in Chapter 1, saw three competing canals: the Leeds and Liverpool, the Huddersfield Narrow and, relevant to Calderdale, the Rochdale.

The Rochdale Canal, the third and final trans-Pennine canal, obtained its Act of Parliament in 1794. The route was from Sowerby Bridge, on the Calder and Hebble Navigation to Castlefield, Manchester, on the Bridgewater Canal, by way of Hebden Bridge and Rochdale, a distance of 32 miles (51km) and ninety-two locks. In 1804, it became the first of the three trans-Pennine canals to be fully opened – perhaps due to the choice of a route over the top of the Pennines, avoiding the problems with tunnel construction that had bedevilled the other two waterways. However, the benefit of being without tunnels speeded up construction but left an everlasting legacy of water supply problems in busy periods. The large number of locks on a relatively short length of canal, which rose to a height of over 600ft (180m), meant that water supply would always be a problem. Seven reservoirs were built specially to service the canal. Locks were made large enough to accommodate broad-gauge (14ft/4m) boats with commercial payloads of up to 70 tons (63.5 tonnes). All the locks were given the same fall, meaning that all gates were the same size, making maintenance easier, and conserved water by using the same amount of water for each lock operation.

Principal cargoes carried included cotton, wool, coal, limestone, timber, salt, agricultural produce and general merchandise. This canal proved to be the most successful of the three trans-Pennine routes and for 120 years its shareholders enjoyed a healthy return on their investment (but somewhat diminished by the end of the First World War).

Collieries were developed around Wakefield from about 1700 and up the valley close to the Calder and Hebble Navigation from 1775. The need to move coal from the pit to the waterway led to the development of an extensive network of wagonways, some being in existence from the 1840s. These early routes were the forerunners of the Lake Lock Railroad, built under the Wakefield Enclosure Act of 1793, which provided for the construction of a railway that could be used by anyone possessing wagons with suitable wheels. The railway commenced at Lake Lock, near Stanley, Wakefield on the Aire and Calder Navigation and ran broadly in a westerly direction to Outwood, a distance of approximately 3 miles (4.8km). In 1804, the route was changed to avoid a steep incline and this resulted in the terminus relocating from Lake Lock to nearby Bottomboat. There were also several branches to collieries and a stone quarry. Extensions were constructed to East Ardsley and Kirkhamgate under a separate Act of Parliament obtained in 1810.

The primary purpose of the line was the carriage of coal from the various coal pits surrounding the line to the Aire and Calder Navigation for shipment elsewhere. Other goods carried included roadstone, timber and burnt lime. The load of three wagons was hauled by one horse with an average gradient of 1 in 70 (1.43 per cent) down to the navigation. The track used edge rails to a gauge of 3ft 4¾in (1,035mm). Goods were charged by toll, initially at 6d per ton (0.9 tonne), subsequently increasing to 10½d per ton (0.9 tonne). In 1807, 110,000 tons (99,790 tonnes) were being carried each year; however, this was not sustained and had reduced to 81,000 tons (73,500 tonnes) by 1819, with a further reduction to 76,000 tons (68,946 tonnes) in 1823. The line gradually declined and was closed in 1836, when the major colliery owner J. & J. Charlesworth built an alternative railway.

A dispute between the railway and William Fenton, which was escalated to be heard at York Assizes, resulted in multi-millionaire Fenton building a separate 4ft 5in gauge wagonway in 1824, following much the same route as the Lake Lock system. Fenton, regarded by many as an eccentric, used bullocks as motive power. He built his first wagonway between Wakefield Bridge and New Park collieries in 1800, duplicating a similar line built by Robert Smithson. Fenton died in 1837 and was reputedly worth £1.5 million. By 1840, his wagonways had ceased operation.

As we saw in Chapter 1, the first railway to connect the West Riding with Lancashire was the Manchester and Leeds Railway Company (M&LR). Proposals to build a railway from Manchester to Leeds originated at about the same time as those for the Liverpool and Manchester Railway (L&MR) and a company was formed in 1825 but, despite the involvement of George Stephenson, the scheme was abandoned, and a reintroduced scheme in 1831 also failed to gain approval.

In 1835, the company was reconstituted with capital fixed at £800,000. Stephenson was again appointed chief engineer and plans were deposited for the following Parliamentary session. The 51-mile (81.6km) route was altered from the earlier proposals to run via Wakefield to Normanton to join the North Midland Railway (NMR), over which it would have running powers from Normanton into Leeds. The eastward diversion was to form easier gradients than previously proposed, but nearer Manchester there were three inclines, each about 4 miles (6.4km) long at 1 in 165 and 1 in 130. In 10 miles (16km) from Manchester, the line would climb 358ft (107m) to a tunnel, 1,705yd (1534.5m) long and two other tunnels of 126 and 280yd (113m/252m). Normanton is some distance east of Wakefield and not on the direct route toward Leeds. However, Parliament seemed determined to limit the number of railways approaching Leeds. Instead, running powers over 9 miles (14km) of the North Midland Railway to Leeds were given and a clause in the Act that should the North Midland Railway fail to build its line, the Manchester and Leeds Railway would have the power to do so.

The Manchester and Leeds Railway Act was given Royal Assent on 4 July 1836. Authorized share capital was £1,300,000 and construction could begin. In order to overcome the challenge of the Pennines, Stephenson proposed a circuitous route from Manchester through Rochdale to Littleborough where a 1.6-mile (2.6km) long tunnel, aptly named Summit Tunnel, saw the beginning of the descent, continuing the line through Walsden and the cotton town of Todmorden into the Upper Colne Valley. From there the line meandered on through another cotton centre, Hebden Bridge, Sowerby Bridge and Horbury, to join the existing North Midland Railway at Normanton to reach Leeds.

Work on the section from Manchester to Littleborough began on 18 August 1837 and on the Summit Tunnel the following year. The tunnel proved much more expensive than planned and took longer to complete. It was nearly finished in December 1839 when a portion of the invert failed, allowing the side walls to move by three-quarters of an inch, requiring them to be rebuilt. Stephenson explained the failure by saying:

> The blue shale through which the excavation passed at that point, was considered so hard and firm, as to render it unnecessary to build the invert very strong there. But shale is always a deceptive material… In this case, falling away like quicklime, it had left the lip of the invert alone to support the pressure of the arch above, and hence its springing inwards and upwards.

At the time of its completion, Summit Tunnel was the longest railway tunnel in the world, at 2,885yd (2,597m). The brickwork varies from five to ten rings in thickness. The total cost was £251,000. There was also a problem at Charlestown Tunnel, between Eastwood and Hebden Bridge. The ground consisted of loose, sandy earth, which gave trouble from the start. On 8 June 1840, it was reported that the masonry inside the tunnel was collapsing and eventually, after much further consideration, the tunnel was abandoned and the line built around the hill at ground level on curves of 12 to 15 chains radius (0.24–0.3km).

On Wednesday 3 July 1839, the line was formally opened from Manchester to Littleborough and two trains, conveying the directors and invited guests, ran as far as Summit Tunnel. On the following day, the line opened to the public over that section; 3,100 passengers were carried. The fare for the 13½ miles (22km) from Manchester to Littleborough was 1st class 4 shillings, 2nd class 2 shillings 6 pence and 3rd class 6 pence. The next section that opened was from Normanton to Hebden Bridge on Monday 5 October 1840.

EDMONDSON CARD TICKETS

The chief booking-clerk at Manchester was Thomas Edmondson, who had invented a machine for printing railway tickets on cards of standard size, numbered progressively, and another machine for stamping the date on each ticket. Edmondson's ticket system and machines came to be used across the whole of the UK rail network, well into the 1970s, almost identical with those first used on the M&LR in 1839.

Former LMS Class 8F 2-8-0, 48321, from Newton Heath depot in Manchester makes its way through Sowerby Bridge on the long climb to Summit Tunnel on 3 May 1968. JOHN HUNT

The North Midland Railway had opened its line to Leeds, using its own terminus at Hunslet Lane on 30 July. As the eastern end of the M&LR was isolated by the uncompleted Summit Tunnel, the NMR provided locomotives for this section until the line was completed. Passengers could now book from Manchester to Leeds, the journey from Littleborough to Hebden Bridge being made in horse-drawn coaches provided by the company. Finally, the line from Hebden Bridge to Summit Tunnel opened on 31 December 1840. The line was inspected by Sir Frederick Smith who sanctioned its opening to the public on behalf of the Board of Trade in February 1841. The main line opening took place on Monday 1 March 1841.

The first timetable showed nine passenger trains each way, except Sundays when there were four. The first weekday eastbound train started from Sowerby Bridge, with the services alternating between all stations and semi-fast, the latter calling at eight intermediate stations compared with fifteen intermediate stops for all-stations trains. The stopping trains took about 3h 20min to and from Leeds, the semi-fast trains took 2h 45min. The timetabled four trains each way on Sundays encountered strong opposition from religious bodies, not least among

Former LMS Class 8F, 48321, passes Mirfield on the Calder Valley line with a loaded coal train comprising over thirty wagons and probably about 400 tons (363 tonnes) of coal, on 3 May 1968. JOHN HUNT

On the lovely summer evening of 2 July 2011, ex-LMS Stanier Black Five, 45305, storms up the grade toward Summit Tunnel through Walsden Station with a returning excursion from Scarborough to Liverpool, aptly named the 'Coast to Coast Express'.

Just three minutes in front of 45305 (shown in the last image) was the regular service between Leeds and Manchester Victoria being handled by Northern Rail's 158860. By the time Rochdale was approached, it is likely that the driver of 45305 was reaching for the brake handle!

A good illustration of the congested nature of the upper Calder Valley. BR Pacific 4-6-2, 70013, makes steady progress passing through Walsden, heading toward the line's summit with an excursion train on 28 April 1968.
JOHN HUNT

the directors. The board was seriously divided with the chairman and two directors resigning in protest against running Sunday trains.

The fact that the line bypassed many important towns is emphasized by the notes in the timetable: Mills Hill (for Oldham); Blue Pitts (for Heywood); Todmorden (for Burnley); Sowerby Bridge (for Halifax); Brighouse (for Bradford) and Cooper Bridge (for Huddersfield).

The Manchester and Leeds Railway: Early Growth

The M&LR quickly achieved substantial profitability, mostly due to the density of population along the route and the fact that, in the early years, much southbound traffic from Manchester was routed this way, owing to disputes affecting the Grand Junction Railway. Despite this, as we have seen, many other important manufacturing locations were in the general area served by the Company and it began to take steps to connect to many of them by building branches or by absorbing other companies. In the West Riding these included:

- Halifax branch, a short line (1¾ miles/2.8km) with severe gradients. Its junction with the main line was at North Dean (later Greetland) and faced Wakefield. The Halifax station was at Shaw Syke and the branch opened on 1 July 1844.
- Huddersfield and Sheffield Junction Railway (H&SJR), a 13-mile (21km) line authorized on 30 June 1845 to connect Huddersfield with the Sheffield, Ashton-under-Lyne and Manchester Railway near Penistone. There was to be a branch to Holmfirth. Amid considerable political tactics, the unbuilt H&SJR was absorbed into the Manchester and Leeds Railway (M&LR) on 27 July 1846. The H&SJR opened to the public on 1 July 1850. At first the MS&LR worked the line, although it was not connected to the M&LR – but, in 1870, the L&YR (successors to the M&LR) began running Sheffield–Huddersfield trains from Penistone.
- The West Riding Union Railway Act of 18 August 1846 authorized a line, supported by the M&LR. The Act required amalgamation with the M&LR within three months. This was done on 17 November 1846; the actual construction of the line being carried out by the M&LR. The section from Low Moor to Mirfield was opened on 18 July 1848, but the more difficult construction from Bradford to Low Moor was delayed until 9 May 1850 and between Mirfield and Halifax to 7 August 1850, with the Sowerby Bridge section opening on 1 January 1852
- The Wakefield, Pontefract and Goole Railway (WP&GR). Seeing potential in expanding eastwards, especially in connecting directly to an east coast port, the M&LR sponsored the promotion of a line from its Wakefield Station. An Act of 31 July 1845 authorized the WP&GR. The planned line ran from the east end of the L&MR Wakefield Kirkgate Station and headed broadly east through Crofton, Featherbridge, Pontefract, Knottingley and Hensall to Goole. The line was opened on 1 April 1848. An Act of 1846 authorized dock improvements at Goole, as well as branches from Pontefract to Methley, opened on 12 September 1849, and from Knottingley to Askern, joining the Great Northern Railway.

The pace of expansion accelerated and, in 1846, it was clear that the company's name was no longer appropriate and the opportunity was taken, when getting Parliamentary authority for further amalgamations, to change the name to the Lancashire and Yorkshire Railway; this took effect by an Act of 9 July 1847.

As the less direct of the routes between Manchester and Leeds, the Calder Valley line had become the route of choice for mineral traffic, particularly coal. The final stages of the climb to Summit Tunnel were challenging from an engineering perspective, with steep gradients greater than 1 in 70 for over half the route to reach the summit level at 749ft (225m) above sea level. This difficult terrain required tunnels, viaducts, embankments and cuttings to enable the line to cling to the steep sides of the narrow valley, which was becoming congested with mills and housing in early Victorian times. To cope with these fearsome gradients, the multitudinous coal trains required powerful engines, often with bankers at the rear, to overcome the gradient.

An additional line was opened from Todmorden to Burnley on 12 November 1849 by the Manchester and Leeds Railway. Its name was not derived from a town or a station, but from a small colliery, signal box and the line summit about midway between Rose Grove and Todmorden, and is known simply as the 'Copy Pit route'. The local service ended in 1965 leaving a daily Leeds–Blackpool train as the only passenger service. Freight services were stopped in 1982 and closure of the line seemed imminent. However, when the National and Provincial Building Society was formed in 1982 from the merger of the Provincial Building Society based in Bradford and the Burnley Building Society this resulted in the relocation of staff working in Burnley to Bradford. The society arranged for a Preston–Bradford Interchange train to assist staff with their new commute. By October 1984 this service was increased to five trains each way between Leeds and Preston with one extended to Blackpool.

In Todmorden, at Hall Royd Junction is a 440yd (400m) section of track known as the Todmorden curve. As Hall Royd Junction was triangular, this curve allowed services from Burnley to reach Manchester via Todmorden. However, regular services ceased in 1965 and the curve was lifted in 1972. Forty years later the reinstatement of the curve was identified as the most important project in Lancashire County Council's 2010 Rail Improvement Schemes report. Network Rail funded a final assessment, completed in May 2011, which concluded that it could be feasible to reinstate the curve but not along the original route as by modern standards this was too sharp. An alternative route was proposed, funding was finally secured and the project was confirmed by the Deputy Prime Minister on 31 October 2011. Construction began in mid-2013, with the first services running on 17 May 2015.

Squeezed into a narrow and typically Pennine valley to the north of Todmorden is Lydgate Viaduct, an attractive structure comprising thirteen arched spans that traverse a geologically challenging landscape to reach Burnley, 9 miles (15km) away. Crossing the viaduct is (now preserved) BR Britannia Pacific 4-6-2, 70013, Oliver Cromwell, on one of its last duties before hauling the end of BR steam 'Fifteen Guinea Special' in 1968. JOHN HUNT

The remains of the winter snow are still in evidence as ex-LMS Class 8F, 2-8-0, 48122, with a sister engine banking at the rear, lifts a heavy coal train up towards Copy Pit from Hall Royd Junction on the Calder Valley line in February 1967, just weeks before withdrawal and scrapping.
JOHN HUNT

There was always a steady procession of west-bound coal trains labouring up to Copy Pit summit in the 1960s. In this image, from February 1968, we see Rose Grove's ex-LMS 8F 2-8-0, 48448, working hard with just such a coal train. This was to be the last year of steam operation on British Railways and 48448 was withdrawn on 27 July.
JOHN HUNT

THE CALDER VALLEY

In most people's understanding, Portsmouth is a town in the south of England. However, regular observers of trains making the climb to Copy Pit summit will be aware of another, much smaller, Portsmouth part-way up the climb. The almost universal choice of locomotive, the ex-LMS 8F 2-8-0, is deployed at the front and the rear of the train in early 1968. Note the sand drag on the left-hand line designed to arrest and derail runaways.
JOHN HUNT

Black Diamonds, *an 8F, banks a loaded coal train toward Copy Pit summit near Cornholme in early 1968.* JOHN HUNT

Summit Tunnel Fire

On 10 December 1984, a major fire occurred in Summit Tunnel, which was of such severity as to warrant relating in detail here.

The tunnel, built in 1840–41, is over one and a half miles long (2,885yd or 2,638m) and is a major engineering feature of the M&LR. Twelve of the fourteen construction shafts, at intervals of approximately 220yd (200m), were left open to help vent smoke and steam from the locomotives that passed through it.

The train involved in this incident was the 01:40 freight train from Haverton Hill, Teesside to Glazebrook oil distribution terminal in Merseyside. It was formed of a BR Class 47 diesel locomotive, 47 125 and thirteen tankers.

At 05:50 on 20 December 1984, the train, carrying more than 1,000,000ltr and weighing 920 tons (835 tonnes) of four-star petrol, entered the tunnel on the Yorkshire (north) side travelling at 40mph (64km/h). One-third of the way through the tunnel, a defective axle bearing derailed the fourth tanker, causing the derailment of those behind. Only the locomotive and the first three tankers remained on the rails. One of the derailed tankers fell on to its side and began to leak petrol into the tunnel. Vapour from the leaking petrol was ignited, probably by the damaged axle box.

The three train crew members could see fire spreading through the ballast beneath the other track in the tunnel, so they left the train and ran the remaining mile to the south portal (where they knew there was a direct telephone connection to the signalman) to raise the alarm.

Crews from both the Greater Manchester Fire Brigade and the West Yorkshire Fire Brigade quickly attended the scene. Co-ordination between the brigades worked well, perhaps because they had both participated in an emergency exercise in the tunnel a month before.

The train crew, showing commendable bravery, were persuaded to return to the train, where they uncoupled the three tankers still on the rails and used the locomotive to drive them out. Greater Manchester Fire Brigade then loaded fire-fighting equipment on to track trolleys and sent a crew with breathing apparatus (BA) in to begin their firefighting operation at the south end of the train. They also lowered hose lines down one of the ventilation shafts to provide a water supply. At the same time, crews from West Yorkshire Fire Brigade entered the tunnel from the opposite end, and began fighting fires in the ballast at the north end of the train.

However, at 09:40, the pressure in one of the heated tankers rose high enough to open its pressure relief valves. The vented vapour caught fire and blew flames on to the tunnel wall. The wall deflected the flames both ways along the tunnel. The BA crews from both brigades decided to evacuate. They managed to leave just before the first explosion rocked the tunnel. The firefighters were saved because the tunnel ventilation shafts 8 and 9 acted as flame vents (a function their designer never envisaged!).

Left to itself, the fire burned as hot as it could. As the walls warmed up and the air temperature in the tunnel rose, all ten tankers discharged petrol vapour from their pressure relief valves. Two tankers melted (at approximately 1,530°C or 2,790°F) and discharged their remaining loads. The fuel supply to the fire was so rich that some of the combustibles were unable to find oxygen inside the tunnel with which to burn; they were instead ejected from vent shafts 8 and 9 as fuel-rich gases that burst into flame when they encountered oxygen in the air outside. At the height of the fire, pillars of flame approximately 45m (148ft) high rose from the shaft outlets on the hillside above.

The gases are estimated to have flowed up these shafts at 50m/s (110mph). Air at this speed is capable of blowing around heavy items: hot projectiles made from tunnel lining (rather like lava bombs from a volcano) were cast out over the hillside. These set much of the vegetation on fire and caused the closure of the A6033 road. In the clean-up operation afterwards, small globules of metal were found on the ground surrounding shaft 9; these had been melted from the tanker walls, swept up with the

BR Class 158 DMU, 158848, leaves the short Winterbutlee Tunnel and approaches Walsden Station on a Manchester to Leeds service on 2 July 2011.

exhaust gases, and dropped out on to the grass around the top of the shaft.

Unable to get close enough to safely fight the fire directly, the fire brigades forced high-expansion foam into ventilation shafts far from the fire. This created blockages that starved the fire of oxygen. By mid-afternoon the next day the inferno was no longer burning, though the fire was by no means extinguished. Petrol continued to leak from the derailed wagons through the tunnel drainage and ballast, and the vapour sporadically reignited when it came into contact with the hot tunnel lining. Two hundred people were evacuated from their homes and workplaces in Walsden in response but were allowed back home the next day. The brigades continued to fight the fire for another two days, until West Yorkshire Fire Brigade issued the stop message just after 18:30 on Christmas Eve. Fire crews remained at the site until 7 January 1985.

Due to the fire, the line between Rochdale and Todmorden was closed and passenger trains between the two stations were replaced by buses. Of the 1,100,000ltr of petrol carried by the train, 275,000ltr were rescued by the train crew when they drove the locomotive and the first three tankers to safety. A further 16,000ltr of petrol were recovered after the fire was extinguished and 809,000ltr burned.

Surprisingly, the damage done by the fire was minimal. Approximately half a mile of track had to be replaced, as did all the electrical services and signalling. The biggest surprise was how well the brick lining had stood up to the fire. Although some bricks in the tunnel and in the ventilation shafts had become so hot that they vitrified and ran like molten glass, most of the brickwork lining of the tunnel was scorched but still serviceable.

The last of the wagons was removed from the tunnel on 1 March 1985. Once British Rail had replaced the track and electrical services, shored up the bases of vent shafts 8 and 9, and filled the two shafts with inert foam (all this took eight months), locals were allowed a once-in-a-lifetime opportunity to walk through the tunnel before train services resumed on 19 August 1985.

Wakefield

After York, Wakefield was the County Town for the West Riding and is the largest settlement in the Calder Valley. The creation of the Aire and Calder Navigation, at the beginning of the eighteenth century, gave access to the North Sea and led to the establishment of an inland port. In 1765, the cattle market was established and became one of the largest in the north of England. The town was a centre for cloth dealing, with its own piece hall, the Tammy Hall, built in 1778.

At the start of nineteenth century, Wakefield was a wealthy market town with a diverse economy and an inland port trading in wool and grain. The establishment of a transport network through the two river navigations and the Barnsley Canal were instrumental in the development of Wakefield as an important market for grain, and more was sold here than at any other market in the north. Grain arrived from far away fields in Norfolk, Cambridgeshire and Lincolnshire. Large warehouses were built on the riverbanks to store grain to supply the fast-growing population of the West Riding. Great quantities of barley were grown in the neighbourhood and several brewers established themselves, including Melbourne's and Beverley's Eagle Breweries. In 1885, more malt was made in Wakefield than anywhere else in the country. The market developed in the streets around the Bull Ring, with the cattle market, between George Street and Ings Road, growing to be one of the biggest in the country. Passenger transport was available for those who could afford it and the establishment of turnpike roads facilitated regular mail coaches to Leeds, London, Manchester, York and Sheffield.

When cloth dealing declined, the local economy diversified still further. Wool-spinning mills using steam power were built by the river, a glassworks in Calder Vale Road, engineering works with strong links to the mining industry, soapworks and brickyards in Eastmoor and boats were built at yards on the Calder. On the outskirts of the town, coal had been dug since the fifteenth century and 300 men were employed in the town's coal pits in 1831.

ORIGINS OF WAKEFIELD

Wakefield can trace its beginnings back to pre-historic times with flint and stone tools. Later, bronze and iron implements, found at Lee Moor and Lupset in the Wakefield area, show evidence of early human activity. This part of Yorkshire was home to the Brigantes until the Roman occupation in AD43. A Roman road from Pontefract passing Streethouse, Heath Common, Ossett Street Side, through Kirklees and on to Manchester crossed the river by a ford at Wakefield near the site of Wakefield Bridge. Wakefield was probably settled by the Angles in the fifth or sixth century and, after AD876, the area was controlled by the Vikings who founded twelve hamlets or 'thorpes' around Wakefield. They divided the area into wapentakes and Wakefield was part of the Wapentake of Agbrigg. The settlement grew near a crossing place on the River Calder around three roads: Westgate, Northgate and Kirkgate.

In 1203, William de Warenne, 5th Earl of Surrey, received a grant for a market in the town. A year later, King John granted the rights for a fair at the feast of All Saints, 1 November and, in 1258, Henry III granted the right for a fair on the feast of Saint John the Baptist, on 24 June. The market was close to the Bull Ring and the church. The townsfolk of Wakefield amused themselves in games and sports, the chief sport in the fourteenth century being archery; the butts in Wakefield were at the Ings, near the river.

During the Wars of the Roses, Richard Plantagenet, Duke of York, was killed on 30 December 1460 in the Battle of Wakefield near Sandal Castle. In medieval times, Wakefield became an inland port on the Calder and centre for the woollen and tanning trades.

At the time of the Civil War, as a Royalist stronghold, Wakefield found itself on the wrong side of the conflict. An attack led by Sir Thomas Fairfax, on 20 May 1643, captured the town for the Parliamentarians. Over 1,500 troops were taken prisoner, along with the Royalist commander.

For 1960s railway enthusiasts, this picture of the entrance to Wakefield steam shed was overwhelming. Look at the locos on display almost in touching distance; look at the Victorian brickwork, which, with the soot and coal dust, gives the place its character and appeal. But watch out, for the dreaded foreman's office door is on the right!
JOHN HUNT

Further into the nineteenth century, more mines were sunk and, by 1869, there were forty-six small mines in Wakefield and the surrounding area. The railways arrived in Wakefield in 1840 in the shape of the Manchester and Leeds Railway, who built a station in Kirkgate.

The original Kirkgate Station was the only station in Wakefield for seventeen years. The booming traffic to Leeds and stations to Manchester, Pontefract and Goole resulted in the construction of a new and larger station in 1854. There were three main platforms, two of which formed an 'island' platform. To cope with the high volumes of freight, mostly coal, passing through, two through lines were provided. The main part of the station was enclosed by a steel and glass roof with an ornate wrought-iron and glass canopy. Despite views to the contrary, the station was handling a significant volume of traffic. Tickets sold for journeys to Wakefield didn't specify which station, so it was not until recently that information has become available. In 2006/7, only 769 tickets

DECLINE OF KIRKGATE STATION

Since the opening of the station in 1840, the station has had a rather chequered career, particularly under British Rail's ownership. Following the Beeching Report, there were plans to close the station altogether. However, public opposition prevented this and, as so often has been the case, BR entered into a period of 'managed neglect'. This neglect went on for many years and the building deteriorated until it was in a poor state of repair. Some demolition work took place in 1972, removing buildings on the island platform and the roof, with its original ironwork canopy that covered the whole station. A wall remains as evidence of these buildings. After this, Kirkgate was listed in 1979. In January 2008, the former goods warehouse was demolished to make way for a depot for Network Rail. In October 2008, part of the station wall collapsed, destroying a parked car.

The station is unstaffed and, despite the presence of CCTV, it has suffered from a crime spree. A rape, a serious assault and several robberies took place there. In July 2009, Kirkgate Station was visited by Secretary of State for Transport, Lord Adonis, who dubbed it 'the worst medium-large station in Britain'. Local consensus was that the state of its facilities discouraged its use.

Wakefield shed toward the end of 1965 showing resident ex-LNER B1 4-6-0, 61024, and War Department 2-8-0, 90336, and others awaiting their next turn of duty.
JOHN HUNT

were recorded as being directly attributable to Kirkgate Station. However, since 2015, the Office of Rail and Road statistics suggest over 520,000 entries and exits with a further 209,000 interchanges.

Fortunately, in the last decade, the station's fortunes have improved. Following a public campaign, plans to redevelop the station were formulated as part of Wakefield Council's plans to redevelop the Kirkgate area. The proposals were funded and improvements were carried out in two phases in 2013 and 2015. These included:

- Removal of life-expired and unused canopies.
- Refurbishment and re-glazing of the Leeds-bound platform canopy.
- Creation of new entrances to the subway.
- Installation of electronic information screens on the platforms and entrance hall.
- Units for new businesses.
- A café.
- A retail outlet.
- Provision of exhibition spaces.
- Meeting rooms for community and local business.
- In addition, Grand Central opened a first-class lounge for its customers in April 2017.

The other station in Wakefield has fared rather better than its earlier rival. Westgate Station, connected to Kirkgate by a spur line, was built by the Bradford, Wakefield and Leeds Railway when it opened its line between Wakefield and junctions near Leeds, on 3 October 1857. The GNR and the L&YR had running powers over the new line, enabling the GNR to route its Doncaster to Leeds trains by this route, using the L&YR from Askern to

Wakefield. The junctions near Leeds were with the Leeds, Bradford and Halifax Junction Railway at Wortley, forming a triangle and enabling through running toward either Leeds or Bradford. This development allowed the GNR to avoid using the hostile Midland Railway track at all, allowing a direct entry to Leeds Central Station, and avoiding the awkward reversal on to the Thirsk line.

Westgate Station, as the name suggests, was built on the south side of Westgate on part of the private estate belonging to wealthy cloth merchant John Milnes; his mid-eighteenth century mansion was partially demolished with its remains incorporated into the station. The station was used for ten years before further developments necessitated its demolition and rebuilding.

A new station opened on the opposite side of Westgate in 1867. It was constructed for the GNR, the Manchester, Sheffield and Lincolnshire and the Lancashire and Yorkshire Railways on the main line from Leeds to Doncaster, which approached Westgate from the north on an embankment before passing through the station and over the bridge in Westgate, which is at the start of a ninety-five-arch viaduct. Built at a cost of £60,000, the station was designed by Leeds engineer J. B. Fraser. A prominent feature was a turreted tower, which, as a result of lobbying by the Wakefield Tradesmen's Association, was converted into a four-faced clock tower in June 1880. The clock's mechanism was designed by the horologist and lawyer Sir Edmund Beckett and made by Potts of Leeds.

Westgate became the main station serving Wakefield because of its location on the main line from Leeds to London. Until the mid-1960s, it had regular services to Bradford Exchange via Batley and Ossett and via Morley Top and to Castleford via the Methley Joint Railway, but these services fell victim to the Beeching cuts between 1964 and 1966. The dire financial state of British Rail in its final years led to deterioration of the fabric of the station buildings, but things improved under Network Rail and plans were prepared for rebuilding.

In 2013, Westgate Station was rebuilt at the northern end of the platforms and the former overflow car park. Key aims of the project, quoting from Graeme Bickerdike in *Rail Engineer*, from 8 July 2013 were to:

- Double the station's retail facilities.
- Improve the forecourt area.
- Provide a station management centre.
- Include staff offices.
- Provide a customer information point.
- Create a first-class waiting room.
- Offer standard-class waiting facilities.
- Install new passenger information technologies.
- Include automated ticket barriers to reduce fare evasion.
- Achieve better pedestrian access to the multi-storey car park and taxi ranks.

Few elements of the modernization programme interfered with the operational railway, except for the installation of additional canopies and the replacement footbridge. Wakefield Westgate was the first newly built station on the East Coast Main Line in decades.

Dewsbury

West of Wakefield along the Calder Valley is Dewsbury. Like Wakefield, Dewsbury can trace its history back to Anglo-Saxon times when, in ecclesiastical terms, it was a place of some importance with towns like Huddersfield, Mirfield and Bradford included in its bailiwick.

In transport terms, a short branch from the Calder and Hebble Navigation reached the town in 1770 and gave access to Manchester and Hull.

As a centre for the shoddy and mungo industries (which recycled woollen items by mixing them with new wool to turn them into heavy blankets and uniforms), Dewsbury was well placed to benefit economically from the Industrial Revolution by virtue of its waterway connection, its location at the centre of the heavy woollen district and its nearby coal mines. The nineteenth century saw a great increase in population, rising from 4,566 in 1801 to around 30,000 by 1890.

DEWSBURY MARKET

Dewsbury Market, hailed as one of the finest in the north, was first established in the area in 1318. A Market Charter was granted by King Edward II to hold a weekly market for local clothiers at nearby Thornhill. The market soon moved to the thriving Dewsbury town centre. When a plague swept through the area, in 1583, it effectively closed down all trading and the market ceased to operate. In 1740, the market was re-established by public demand and, in 1904, the magnificent Market Hall was built. The traders who previously occupied the area in the town centre Market Place moved toward the fine architecture of the Market Hall. The area was famous as the 'Heavy Woollen District' due to the manufacture of quality blankets, coats and military uniforms. The street through the open-market area, known as Cloth Hall Street, reflects this era of history in the area.

Throughout the Middle Ages, Dewsbury retained a measure of importance in ecclesiastical terms, collecting tithes from as far away as Halifax in the mid-fourteenth century. John Wesley visited the area five times in the mid-eighteenth century and the first Methodist Society was established in 1746. Centenary Chapel on Daisy Hill commemorates the centenary of this event and the Methodist tradition remained strong in the town.

THE CHARTISTS

In the 1830s, Dewsbury was a centre of Chartist agitation. In August 1838, after a speech by Chartist leader Fergus O'Connor, a mob of between 5,000 and 7,000 people besieged the Dewsbury Poor Law Guardians in the town's Royal Hotel. The mob was dispersed by troops.

Trouble flared again, in 1840, when radical agitators seized control of the town and troops were stationed there to maintain order. This radical tradition left a legacy in the town's political life – its first elected MP in 1867 was John Simon, a Jewish lawyer from Jamaica and a Liberal. There was a tradition of firing the 'ten o'clock' gun, which dates from 1815 and was a hangover from the Luddite problems. It was fired from Wormald and Walker's Mill to reassure that all was well. It could be heard all over the area. Eventually, the actual gun was replaced with a specially made firework, but the tradition was discontinued in 1983 with the closure of the mills. The mills were family businesses and continued manufacturing after the wool crisis in 1950–51, which saw Australian sheep farmers begin to charge higher prices. However, the recovery of the late 1960s was reversed by the 1973 oil crisis and the textile industry in Dewsbury declined, with only bed manufacturing remaining a large-scale employer.

The town's rapid expansion and commitment to industrialization resulted in social instability. In the early nineteenth century, Dewsbury was a centre of Luddite opposition to mechanization, by which workers retaliated against the mill owners who had installed textile machinery and, as they saw it, had taken their livelihoods. The Luddite groups went on the rampage and smashed the machines that threatened their way of life.

Dewsbury Passenger Stations

The original railway station for Dewsbury was a mile away from the town centre at Thornhill but, notwithstanding this distance, was still called Dewsbury. It was built by the M&LR and opened in 1840. It was built on the main line and had the status of such, not least because of its substantial adjacent goods-handling facility, but within ten years of having been built, its importance was somewhat reduced by the arrival of town centre competition. This was a line built by the Leeds, Dewsbury and Manchester Railway, which was absorbed by the London and North Western Railway prior to opening. It ran from the M&LR at Dewsbury Junction, Ravensthorpe, through a new station in Dewsbury at Wellington Road, although it was simply called Dewsbury and was opened on 18 September 1848. It was subsequently named Dewsbury Wellington Road from 2 June 1924 until 20 February 1969, when it reverted to the original name. The 1840 Dewsbury Station was renamed Thornhill from September 1848.

Conscious of the traffic that was now flowing through its competitor's new station, the Lancashire and Yorkshire, after waiting a decent time, built a branch to the town from its Manchester and Leeds line in 1866 to a third station, Dewsbury

Market Place. It was only moderately successful and was closed to passengers by the LMSR in 1930 and to goods traffic by British Railways in 1961.

Also, not to be outdone by its competitors, the Great Northern opened its Dewsbury branch from Wakefield in 1874, initially to a terminal station, Dewsbury Central, but this became a through station when the line was extended to Batley in 1880. The station had a single, large, island platform with a glass roof accessed from below through an entrance on Crackenedge Lane. This line and the station fell victim to the Beeching axe and closed on 7 September 1964.

The Midland Railway had ambitions to build a new line between Sheffield and Bradford and, indeed, by the end of the nineteenth century, much of the route was in place. The objective was to avoid the congested area around Leeds. Fearful of the competition, the Lancashire and Yorkshire gave the Midland running powers on its lines, so the scheme was never completed. The line only reached as far as Dewsbury, where it terminated at Savile Town goods yard, opened in 1906.

Dewsbury was remarkable for having, at one time, four passenger stations and a dedicated goods station. That one has survived and prospered, must be testament to the virtues of rail travel that allows the movement of large numbers of people to and from their places of work or business swiftly and at an affordable price.

Halifax

The town's nineteenth-century wealth came from the cotton, wool and carpet industries and, like most other Yorkshire towns, it had many weaving mills, some of which have now been lost or converted to alternative use.

In 1853, one of the country's best-known building societies was started under the title of the Halifax Permanent Benefit Building and Investment Society. Today, the bank operates as a trading name of HBOS, part of the Lloyds Banking Group. Colonel Edward Akroyd of Halifax established the Yorkshire Bank in the town on 1 May 1859. It is now based in

HALIFAX – EARLY HISTORY

There is no mention of the town in the Domesday Book, although it is believed that a settlement existed here from about AD900. However, by the twelfth century, the township had become the centre of a very large ecclesiastical parish that extended from Heptonstall in the west to Brighouse in the east. Halifax Minster dates from this period, having been started in the twelfth century and finished in 1438.

The coat of arms of Halifax includes the chequers from the original coat of arms of the Earls Warenne, who held the town during Norman times (1066–1348).

Punishment in Halifax for wrongdoers was notoriously harsh – the town was known and feared for its gibbet, an early form of guillotine used to execute criminals by decapitation, last used in 1650. A replica has been erected on the original site in Gibbet Street. The notoriety of the punishment in Halifax was recorded in the *Beggar's Litany* by John Taylor (1580–1654), a prayer whose text included 'From Hull, Hell and Halifax, good Lord deliver me'. Beggars were afraid of Hull because they were liable to be press-ganged and sent to sea, of Hell for obvious reasons and of Halifax because there was the fearsome gibbet – where anyone caught stealing goods over a certain value was summarily beheaded.

Leeds but was originally known as the West Riding Penny Savings Bank.

The success of the Aire and Calder Navigation led to lobbying for similar treatment of the Calder and Hebble rivers, with a view to making a transport artery from Wakefield to Sowerby Bridge to secure better transport links to the town for the import of corn and wool. To move forward with the proposal, a meeting of the Union Club was held in Halifax on 2 September 1756. The meeting agreed to underwrite the cost of a survey and obtaining the necessary act of Parliament, and invited the civil engineer John Smeaton to make a new survey, which he did in late 1757. He produced a scheme that involved dredging shoals, making 5¾ miles (9.2km) of new cuts, the building of twenty-six locks to overcome the rise of 178ft (54m) between Wakefield and the Halifax Brook, and the construction of a reservoir at Salterhebble bridge. An Act was obtained on 9 June 1758,

Situated on the M&LR's main line, between Mytholmroyd and Sowerby Bridge, is Luddendenfoot. Working hard on the upgrade is ex-LMS Class 8F 2-8-0, 48321, in May 1968. Steam traction was very much in its last days with the last steam trains running the following August. 48321, a resident of Newton Heath depot, was withdrawn about a month after this image was captured. JOHN HUNT

for the entire route. Construction started in November 1759, with Smeaton acting as engineer.

The Act was the first Navigation Act to include a clause that limited dividends, insisting that tolls should be reduced if the dividend exceeded 10 per cent. Construction of the initial phase was finished in 1770 at a total cost of around £75,000.

The Navigation prospered, with dividends rising steadily from 5 per cent in 1771 to 13 per cent in 1792. Under the terms of the Act of Parliament, tolls were reduced when the dividend exceeded 10 per cent, the first such reduction occurring in 1791. Improvements continued and were funded by making calls on the original shareholders. This provided a way to increase their income without exceeding the 10 per cent dividend limit. Another stimulus to trade was provided by the Rochdale Canal, which opened up a through route from Sowerby Bridge to Manchester from 1804. A new Act of Parliament was obtained on 31 March 1825 authorizing the raising of £50,000 for the purpose of constructing a 1¾-mile (2.8km) branch along the route of the River Hebble, from Salterhebble to the centre of Halifax, terminating near the railway station at Bailey Hall. The terminus was 100ft (30m) above the level of the canal at Salterhebble, the branch requiring a total of fourteen locks. It opened fully in 1828.

A mere twelve years later, the Manchester and Leeds Railway opened in 1840, but remained in the Calder Valley 200ft (61m) below Halifax, giving the Calder and Hebble more time to build their goods traffic on the newly opened Halifax branch canal. This meant that intending railway passengers and goods' forwarders had to start their journeys at either Sowerby Bridge or Elland.

By 1831, the population had reached 15,382 and cotton manufacture had begun to erode the local monopoly of wool, which had lasted for six hundred years. In this early part of the Railway Age, the Industrial Revolution was proceeding apace and the effect on the population was so damaging that the average life-expectancy was no more than twenty-six years.

Whilst its main line was still under construction, the M&LR obtained an Act on 1 July 1839 for a short branch from North Dean (later re-named Greetland) to Shaw Syke in Halifax. The Act stipulated that the line was to be constructed 'as speedily as possible' and completed within three years. This was largely ignored by the M&LR who eventually opened the single-track line to traffic in 1844. The company still faced complaints from the public over poor connections to Manchester and from the staff over the difficulties of working trains on the line over gradients as severe as 1 in 44.

In 1847, M&LR merged with others to become the Lancashire and Yorkshire Railway (L&YR). In 1850, the L&YR extended the line eastwards from Halifax through Beacon Hill Tunnel to Hipperholme,

Lightcliffe and thence by Low Moor to Bradford and Leeds. The company also constructed a more direct line from Halifax to Sowerby Bridge in 1852, when the twenty-three-arch viaduct at Copley came into use. These new lines led to the line being extended between 1850 and 1855 from Shaw Syke to the site of the present station in Horton Road, Shaw Syke becoming a goods depot.

The opening of the Leeds, Bradford and Halifax Junction Railway (LB&HJR), in 1854, allowed the GNR to use its previously agreed running powers over the L&YR to run into Halifax. The extra traffic necessitated a new station on the Horton Road site, which came into use on 23 June 1855. Direct services from Halifax to Manchester were introduced in 1863 and the original branch from North Dean (later Greetland) to Dryclough Junction was widened to two tracks.

In 1865, the L&YR got Parliamentary approval for a branch from North Dean (later Greetland) to Stainland. The construction wasn't rushed and it took ten years before the line opened. Another branch authorized at the same time was from Sowerby Bridge to Rishworth. This was constructed to main-line standards, as it was envisaged as the first stage of a cut-off line direct to Littleborough, passing through a 4-mile (6.4km) tunnel under Blackstone Edge shortening the Calder Valley route by about 5 miles (8km). As part of the scheme, the existing Sowerby Bridge Station was moved to the east by about half a mile (0.8km) in 1876. Two years later, the line reached Ripponden, much delayed by the difficulties encountered in boring Ripponden Tunnel, a 593yd (540m) structure. This short tunnel had cost an 'eye watering' £40,000 and didn't bode well for the 4-mile (6.4km) structure through Blackstone Edge. The line reached Rishworth in 1881 but, fearful of the eventual cost, the L&YR 'pulled the plug' and abandoned the scheme.

The population of Halifax was growing year on year as the industrialization of the town proceeded. In 1861, it stood at just over 37,000, but ten years later, with some help from boundary changes, it had grown to 65,500. A major employer was Crossley's Dean Clough Mills, which had grown from employing 300 in 1837 to 5,000 in 1870, and had styled themselves as 'the largest carpet factory in the world'. John Crossley was one of the leading promoters of a line from Halifax to Keighley and, although the original proposal was thrown out by Parliament in 1864, with the help of the GNR, the Queensbury lines were eventually built, as we saw in the last chapter.

The last extension to the local network was High Level Railway, which was opened in 1890. This started from Holmfield, tunnelled under Ovenden and emerged in the Wheatley Valley, where there were sidings to Samuel Webster's Brewery. The continual extension of Halifax as a town had led to development of land higher and higher up the western slopes of the Hebble valley. One-hundred and thirty mills had been established and some 80,000 tons (72,575 tonnes) of coal were being dragged up the steep roads annually to supply them. This was one of the reasons for the incorporation, in 1884, of the Halifax High Level and North and South Junction Railway. Its promoters, no doubt wearing rose-tinted spectacles, saw the line as a vital link in a new route for Midland Anglo-Scottish Expresses, which would reach a high-level station in George Street, Halifax, via a projected expansion of the Hull and Barnsley through Huddersfield and then continue over the GNR route to Keighley. This dream, of course, collapsed and the works were restricted to a branch from Homefield to St. John's costing £300,000 for a 3-mile (4.8-km) railway. This high cost was brought about by an 810yd (737m) tunnel through solid rock and a ten-arch viaduct. The gradients were steep, with a short length at 1 in 35 at Holmfield and a longer length at 1 in 50 up to Pellon. The line was worked jointly by the L&YR and the GNR, with the latter providing the passenger service that commenced in 1890.

Sadly, all of the branch lines in the Halifax area have succumbed to competition from buses, the private motor car or the 'Beeching axe'. Where once there were six platforms, now only two are provided; the magnificent Horton Road Station building has been put to other uses and the services now provided reach Huddersfield, Manchester Victoria, Blackpool, Bradford, Leeds, York and Hull.

CHAPTER 10

Huddersfield

Like many parts of the West Riding in the early period of the Industrial Revolution, bulk transport of materials and fuel was waterborne. We saw in Chapter 1 how frustration with the slow progress of the construction of the Leeds and Liverpool Canal led to the formation of the Huddersfield Canal Company, which obtained its Act of Parliament in 1794. The proprietors of this company were a group of merchants in Ashton, Manchester, who proposed a new waterway from the Ashton Canal at Dukinfield to run in an easterly direction through Stalybridge, over the border into the West Riding at Diggle and then via Marsden to Huddersfield, where a junction with Sir John Ramsden's Canal would be made. Although a relatively short canal, less than 20 miles (32km), many engineering difficulties needed to be overcome. Not least of these was the construction of a tunnel under the watershed, Standedge Tunnel.

By the 1960s, the Huddersfield Narrow Canal was derelict, as seen in this view at Marsden, close to the tunnel entrance. On the adjacent railway, ex-LMS Black Five 4-6-0, 45046, drifts down through the station with a train of vans. The Huddersfield Narrow Canal was subsequently fully restored and re-opened to navigation.
JOHN HUNT

ORIGINS OF HUDDERSFIELD

Huddersfield can trace its history back for 4,000 years. There is evidence to suggest that Castle Hill, a major local landmark, was the site of an Iron Age hill fort constructed in the early Iron Age, around 555BC, taking up the whole hilltop. Modifications were made around AD43 to improve the defences, probably in response to the threat from the Roman invaders.

These same Roman invaders felt obliged to construct a defensive fort at Slack. This was a *castellum* near Outlane, to the west of Huddersfield and was built around AD79. The fort was intended to defend the Pennine section of Roman road from Chester (Deva Victrix) to York (Eboracum). Archaeological digs suggest that the fort was constructed of turf and wood. Outside the fort walls was a stone bath-house, which was extended around AD104 and again in AD120. A small settlement of wooden huts grew up outside the fort.

In Anglo-Saxon times, Huddersfield became a market town with a market cross, unsurprisingly, on the Market Place. Until 1322, the manor of Huddersfield was owned by the de Lacy family but reverted to royal ownership in that year. In 1599, a William Ramsden bought the manor and the Ramsden family continued to own it until 1920, the manor being known as the Ramsden Estate. The Cloth Hall was built in Huddersfield in 1766 by Sir John Ramsden, 3rd Baronet, and the 4th Baronet was responsible for Sir John Ramsden's Canal in 1780.

There was industrial unrest in the early nineteenth century when traditional weavers feared for their living as mechanization was introduced. The Luddites were responsible for attacks on mills in the area, even going to the extent of murdering at least one mill-owner. The government stationed a platoon of soldiers in the town to repress these attacks and, eventually, the movement faded out, but not before Parliament began to increase welfare provision for those out of work and to introduce regulations to improve conditions in the mills.

Canal (Sir John Ramsden's Canal) could take wider but shorter craft, as used on the Calder and Hebble Navigation. Goods, therefore, had to be trans-shipped between the two at Huddersfield. This enforced double-handling increased costs to unacceptable levels.

However, despite these difficulties the canal did enjoy a short period of relative prosperity until the 1840s, when it became prey to the intensely competitive railway companies. As early as 1825, it had been suggested that the canal should be filled in and the tunnel used for a railway. The Manchester and Leeds Railway attempted to purchase the canal so as to gain a monopoly on the local carrying trade. The Canal Company rejected this offer but, in 1844, decided to sell out to the Huddersfield and Manchester Railway, which had been locally promoted earlier in the year to build a line from Cooper Bridge on the M&LR to a junction at Stalybridge with the Sheffield, Ashton-under-Lyne and Manchester Railway (SA&MR). The combined undertaking became

TUNNELLING DELAYS AT STANDEDGE

Standedge Tunnel became the highest, longest (5,451yd or 4,984m) and deepest canal tunnel in Britain. Its construction came close to bankrupting the company, although the company's ability to get its shareholders to meet their calls left much to be desired, leaving them in a constant cash-flow deficit. Benjamin Outram was appointed the consulting engineer after his report in October 1793 estimated the cost of the canal and tunnel at £178,478. Nicholas Brown surveyed the route. In the event, nearly £400,000 was spent, equivalent to £32 million today. Standedge Tunnel alone cost nearly £124,000 or around £10 million today.

Nicholas Brown, who surveyed the route, was appointed as surveyor, book-keeper and superintendent in July 1794 at a salary of £315 a year. Doubt has been cast on the wisdom of this appointment as Brown was inexperienced in this kind of work and was effectively the resident engineer for a major civil engineering project stretching over 20 miles (32km). That the workload was probably too much for him can be seen by the errors of organization that he made, the disputes with adjoining landowners and mill proprietor, and the generally slow progress. In 1801, Outram resigned and Brown was dismissed.

Parts of the works were already in use but the tunnelling was still interminably slow. In 1806, the company invited one of the most experienced civil engineers in the land, Thomas Telford, to inspect the works and come up with a plan to complete them. This he did and by following his plan to the letter, they were able to declare the whole route, from Ashton to Huddersfield, complete by the end of 1810. Formal opening took place in April 1811.

The canal was built for 70-ft (21m) long narrowboats, whilst the Huddersfield Broad known as the Huddersfield and Manchester Railway and Canal Company (H&MRCC).

This was a smart move by the fledgling railway company and by agreeing to build the railway roughly parallel to the course of the canal, would enable massive savings in the construction costs to be achieved. This was particularly so in constructing a new tunnel under Standedge, where the old shafts could be re-used and the excavated spoil could be removed by boat.

By this time the railway mania was in full swing and others were casting covetous eyes over the H&MRCC route. The SA&MR, having failed to get Parliamentary approval for a line through Standedge to Huddersfield in 1843, still had visions of gaining control of the area's rail network by means of a merger with the H&MRCC. The prize for the SA&MR was the access to Leeds that this could give and so enable competition with the much longer M&LR. It almost worked! When put to a vote of the H&MRCC shareholders in 1846, the merger was narrowly defeated by a mere 613 votes.

A provisional committee was established for the formation of another railway company, the Huddersfield and Sheffield Junction Railway (H&SJR), which was planned to leave the H&MRCC west of Huddersfield at Paddock and join the SA&MR at Penistone and thence to Sheffield via Barnsley. The SA&MR had managed to get no fewer than five directors on this committee with the intention of a merger. Unfortunately, the SA&MR dithered and the M&LR saw the chance of getting into Huddersfield. Despite intense Parliamentary opposition from the SA&MR, the M&LR was able to get Parliamentary approval to absorb the infant H&SJR in 1846. The final piece of the jigsaw to fall into place was when the M&LR obtained running powers over the H&MRCC from Huddersfield to Paddock in 1847, allowing access to its previously isolated H&SJR line. In return, the M&LR agreed not to oppose the amalgamation of the H&MRCC and the Leeds, Dewsbury & Manchester Railway (LD&M) with the London and North Western.

To make this chain of events easier to follow, it might be helpful if the consequences of the fallout from the railway mania, which led to several mergers into larger companies, is outlined. These included:

- From 16 July 1846 – The London North Western Railway formed from: the London and Birmingham Railway; the Grand Junction Railway; the Manchester and Birmingham Railway; the Leeds, Dewsbury and Manchester Railway and the Huddersfield and Manchester Railway.
- From 1 January 1847 – The Manchester Sheffield and Lincolnshire Railway from: the Sheffield, Ashton-under-Lyne and Manchester Railway and the authorized, but not built, Great Grimsby and Sheffield Junction Railway (Gainsborough to Grimsby); the Sheffield and Lincolnshire Junction Railway (Sheffield to Gainsborough); The Sheffield and Lincolnshire Extension Railway (Retford to Lincoln).
- From 9 July 1847 – The Lancashire and Yorkshire Railway from: the Manchester and Leeds Railway; Ashton, Stalybridge and Liverpool Junction Railway and the Wakefield, Pontefract and Goole Railway.

The 1846 agreement between the H&MRCC and the M&LR also included a clause making the construction of Huddersfield Station and the line west to Paddock to be at the joint expense of the two companies. This outbreak of newfound harmony heralded a complete change from the acrimonious relationship of only a few years earlier. To mark this new accord, it was decided to produce a station of architectural merit and to this end a well-regarded York architect, James Piggott Pritchett (the elder), was commissioned to carry out the design. The tenders for the construction amounted to £20,000 (about £2.4m at 2020 prices), a not insignificant sum, but the end result was well worth waiting for. The companies jointly accepted the proposal and work began with the laying of the foundation stone on 9 October 1846 by Lord Fitzwilliam. A public holiday was declared and the church bells were rung from dawn to dusk.

Construction of the station proceeded apace and one wing was completed by August 1847 when the

The very impressive facade of the joint LNW and L&YR station in Huddersfield. British Railway planned to demolish this building but Huddersfield Town Council would have none of it; they stepped in and bought the freehold. The statue in front of the station is of former Prime Minister Harold Wilson, one of the town's most famous sons. RACHEL NEWALL

Standing on Huddersfield shed, and looking very smart after a recent visit to Derby works in March 1961, is ex-LMS Fowler Class 4P 2-6-4T, 42317. This proved to be the last works' visit for the engine and it was withdrawn in August 1965. JOHN HUNT

first section of the line was opened. This was the section that would yield the best revenue in the early months and was from Huddersfield to Heaton Lodge Junction on the Lancashire and Yorkshire Railway (L&YR), giving access to Leeds by the old M&LR route. Initially, a single line of rails with only a passenger service was provided. By November, a second line was complete when a goods service became available. Huddersfield Station was completed in October 1850.

In addition to the impressive station facade, the L&NWR constructed a locomotive depot to the

Approaching the western end of Standedge Tunnel at Diggle, on 22 July 2011, is First Trans Pennine Express Class 185, 185124, with a service from Manchester Airport to Middlesbrough.

north-east of the station. It came into use in 1849 and was closed in January 1967. Normally it had around thirty engines allocated to it, but in the final year this had reduced to about half a dozen.

As noted above, construction of the L&NWR–H&MRCC line began in 1846 in an easterly direction toward Heaton Lodge. Work also commenced to build the line up into the Pennines at the same time. The route was a steady climb up the Colne Valley on a ruling gradient of 1 in 105 through Paddock, Slaithwaite and Marsden, where construction of the Standedge Tunnel commenced. The contractor appointed was Thomas Nicholson, who had built the original Woodhead Tunnel and, indeed, the tunnel was originally named after him as the Nicholson Tunnel. The presence of the canal tunnel simplified construction. The original shafts were used again and passageways cut through to the canal tunnel to enable the excavated spoil to be removed by barge. There were thirteen of these interconnecting passageways (known as adits) and many were retained to facilitate drainage from the railway tunnel into the canal. The new tunnel ran parallel to, and to the south of, the canal tunnel at a slightly higher level. The tunnel was driven and lined by up to 1,953 navvies working thirty-six faces. The tunnel advanced at up to 85yd (78m) per week. The relative ease of construction led to the tunnel being completed in just over two years, considerably shorter than the Woodhead Tunnel, which, with the same contractor, took seven years. The structure was 3 miles 57yd long (4,800m) and was level throughout. Operationally, this was convenient, as it was the only level stretch on the whole railway where water troughs could be provided.

When the tunnel opened, trains were accompanied on the single line through the tunnel by a pilot man or pilot engine and their re-emergence was communicated between signal boxes situated at either end by a telegraph system.

This 1848 tunnel soon became a bottleneck for rail traffic between Huddersfield and Manchester. Even before its completion, plans were in consideration for a second tunnel alongside it. When the London and North West Railway (L&NWR) was satisfied that the economic case was clear, Thomas Nelson was awarded the construction contract. As with the first tunnel, the canal tunnel was linked to the second by twenty-one adits that passed underneath Nicholson's Tunnel, allowing spoil to be removed by boat. In February 1871, the 3-mile 57yd long (4,880m) second rail tunnel, to the south of the first, was opened.

Emerging from Standedge Tunnel at Marsden, heading an eastbound mixed freight train on 2 May 1968 is ex-LMS Class Black Five 4-6-0, 45406, of Speke Junction. The position of the three railway tunnels is quite clear in this picture and the entrance to the canal tunnel is behind the cottages on the right.
JOHN HUNT

Even two tunnels could not provide sufficient capacity to satisfy demand and, in 1890, the L&NWR embarked on providing four tracks on most of the line, which required constructing a further, twin-track tunnel. Construction was done under the guidance of A. A. MacGregor, the L&NWR chief engineer, and carried out by 1,800 men who lived in the paper mills at Diggle and fifty-four wooden huts near the eastern side. Once again the tunnel was driven from adits, this time thirteen adits were connected to the first railway tunnel. The canal tunnel was extended at the Diggle end to accommodate the third rail tunnel, which ran close past it. For most of its length, the new bore is to the north of the canal tunnel, but passes over the canal tunnel just inside each tunnel entrance. When the work was completed, the tunnel was 3 miles 60yd (4,883m) long. About 25 million bricks, which were mostly produced locally, were used in the tunnel lining. On 1 August 1894, the new tunnel was passed for use by HM Inspector of Railways, Major Yorke.

The opening of the H&MRCC route by the L&NWR was the catalyst for expansion of the industries up the Colne Valley to Marsden, originally established to take advantage of the Huddersfield Canal. The area led the West Riding in the introduction of the Jacquard loom, specializing in tweeds and woollens for the popular market and supplying much of the material for the cloth caps of the northern working man.

In the mid-eighteenth century, Huddersfield had been less than half the size of Halifax but, from the early nineteenth century, it started to pull ahead with the town being serviced by a waterway and later by a trunk railway route. Population grew

Situated in the western suburbs of Huddersfield is the Colne Valley settlement of Longwood. A substantial passenger station was provided by the L&NWR and it is seen in this image in its dying days before closure in 1968. Drifting down the valley toward Huddersfield is ex-LMS Class Black Five 4-6-0, 45406, of Speke Junction. JOHN HUNT

Passing through the impressive earthworks of Longwood Cutting, Huddersfield, in May 1968 is ex-LMS Black Five 4-6-0, 45046, with a partially fitted freight train.
JOHN HUNT

from 13,284 in 1821 to 30,880 a mere thirty years later. The town gained a name for fine worsted cloth and was well laid out by the Ramsden family who were virtually the sole proprietors. Boundary changes in 1868 made the town of Huddersfield into a Borough, the increased size seeing a further jump in population from 34,877 in 1861 to 70,253 by 1871. The local dyeing trade grew into a successful chemical industry, which, in turn, produced further traffic for the railway.

In the summer of 1869, the single platform at the station is reported to have handled 160 trains.

It is difficult to understand why the owning L&YR and L&NWR companies didn't respond earlier to the overcrowding crisis. For a station with such an elegant facade, it must have been a major anticlimax to find so little provision for the traveller. The tunnel at one end accentuated the bottleneck. Safety standards had been allowed to slip and the station was averaging a major accident every two years. The Board of Trade got to hear of this and condemned the layout, instructing the companies to make improvements. Despite this condemnation, it was not until 1878 that agreement was reached to enlarge the station. The improvements consisted of an island platform with an overall roof and removal of all goods traffic to new, separate facilities away from the passenger station. Unfortunately, the improvements were delayed in August 1885 when part of the new overall roof collapsed killing four men. Despite this set-back, the enlarged station was completed in October 1886.

Services provided comprised main-line expresses from Newcastle, Hull and Leeds to Manchester and Liverpool. Despite its stewardship of the West Coast Main Line, the L&NWR did not actively seek London traffic from Huddersfield and even at the end of the nineteenth century, there was only one through train from the town to the capital.

With the general fall-off in rail traffic through the twentieth century, contraction was inevitable. On 31 October 1966, the two single-line Standedge tunnels were closed and long sections of the quadruple track layout in the West Riding were taken out of use. The graceful and distinctive Huddersfield Station facade was proposed for demolition by British Rail in 1966 but, fortunately, the Huddersfield Corporation was able to buy both the facade and platform 1 and thereby save the town's most elegant building to mark the centenary of the Borough in 1968.

Huddersfield and Sheffield Junction Railway

Whereas the Huddersfield and Manchester Railway (later L&NWR) was built with the 'grain' of the terrain that it passed through and was able to minimize the need for expensive structures (give or take a tunnel or two), the Huddersfield and Sheffield Junction Railway had to cut across the grain of the land, tunnelling through minor watersheds and striding across the tributary valleys of the rivers Colne, Dearne and Don before joining the Manchester, Sheffield and Lincolnshire Railway at Huddersfield Junction, Penistone. In all, 2¼ miles (3.6km) of tunnels, four major viaducts and fifty-seven bridges were needed. From its junction with the H&MRCC between Huddersfield and Springwood tunnels, the line turns south and curves across Paddock Viaduct comprising fifteen arches and four iron spans 70ft (22m) above the Colne; the short Yew Green Tunnel is next, followed quickly by Lockwood Viaduct with thirty-four arches towering 136ft (41.5m) over the River Holme. For a while, the line follows the valley of the Holme until the longest tunnel on the line is encountered. This is Thurstonland Tunnel and it is 1,631yd (1,480m) long. Before Penistone is reached, there are two more tunnels and two more viaducts.

Emerging from Huddersfield South Tunnel on 2 September 1967 is ex-LMS Jubilee class, 4-6-0, 45593, Kolhapur, with a train to Manchester. Note the beginning of the junction for the L&YR line to Penistone in the bottom right of the picture.
JOHN HUNT

Initially, from the opening in 1850, the line was worked by the MS&LR and, from 1857, it retimed all its trains to connect with the MS&LR's new service from King's Cross to Manchester. This was further improved in 1859 when, in conjunction with the GNR, through coaches, working from King's Cross to Huddersfield, were inaugurated. An Act of the same year stipulated that the L&YR must provide 'all reasonable facilities' for this traffic. Seven years later, on 30 July 1866, the Midland was authorized to run into Huddersfield from Beighton on the former North Midland line via Sheffield Victoria and Penistone with additional accommodation being sanctioned at Huddersfield station.

In July 1870, the L&YR began to work forward the Sheffield to Huddersfield trains from Penistone and, in 1882, in collaboration with the MS&LR, provided a new service from Huddersfield to King's Cross. In the same year, the L&YR worked the Sheffield to Huddersfield trains throughout. Over the years, the Penistone line had gained in importance as a trunk route and the final stage in this development came in May 1900 when a new service was introduced from Bradford Exchange to Marylebone over the Great Central's new London Extension. This was worked over the line by the L&YR as far as Sheffield.

The Penistone line remains in use to the present day and, although built as double-track, it was singled following modernization works in 1983 and 1989 (aside from a pair of crossing loops at Penistone and between Stocksmoor and Shepley). There was a threat of closure in the 1970s when passenger numbers fell to an all-time low and there was a risk of support from the Passenger Transport Executive being withdrawn. However, this did not happen and the line is now part of the Community Rail network and enjoys patronage by more than a million passengers a year.

Huddersfield was unusual in the industrial West Riding in that it had more branch lines than any other local area and three of these were hosted by the H&SJR. In the upper part of the Holme Valley a branch left the main line south of Brockholes and ran to Holmfirth. The line was double-track and was built at the same time as the H&SJR main line, opening in 1850. There was one intermediate station at Thongs Bridge. The branch closed to passengers in 1959.

MELTHAM MILLS HALT

For a time, there was an unusual station, Meltham Mills Halt, which was erected solely for the use of employees of Jonas Brooke's Thread Mills, in return for the sale of land on which to build the railway. Tickets were issued at the Mill office only and the halt remained in use until September 1934. Traffic can never have lived up to expectations and the branch closed in 1949.

A branch to Meltham left the main line just north of Lockwood Viaduct and climbed at a steady 1 in 60 through not unattractive woodland pausing at Netherton and Healey House stations on the way. The construction of the line was not without its problems and the opening was delayed by a partial tunnel collapse, a cutting slip and embankment subsidence. Nevertheless, the single-line branch was opened in 1869.

The third branch from the H&SJR was constructed not only for the obvious reason of tapping into the traffic from collieries and mills in the area, but also to honour an obligation given to the Midland Railway. This obligation arose from an agreement between the MR and the L&YR whereby the MR did not proceed with its proposal to construct a line from Barnsley to Kirkburton in exchange for running powers to Huddersfield via Penistone. The MR had given an undertaking to serve the town of Clayton West en route and this undertaking was to be discharged by the L&YR, as part of the agreement with the MR, by constructing a short line from near Shepley to Clayton West. The Act was procured in 1866, but the L&YR dragged its feet somewhat in constructing the line, which was not opened until 1879.

Strategically, the L&YR built the branch with bridges and a tunnel wide enough for double-track, expecting to build a 3-mile (4.8km) extension from Clayton West to its Barnsley branch; authorization for this was obtained in 1893. It was foreseen that, in conjunction with the Retford, Rotherham and

It was pretty unusual to see a former Southern Railway Pacific in the West Riding of Yorkshire in 2011. However, West Coast Railways, operator of the weekly excursion from Crewe to Scarborough, found itself with a locomotive crisis in the north of England and so unrebuilt Battle of Britain Class Pacific, 34067, Tangmere, was summoned from Southall depot in London to undertake the journey.

Barnsley Railway, also authorized in 1893, greater access to the South Yorkshire coalfield for the L&YR could be offered to the GNR in exchange for direct access to Huddersfield. Unfortunately, this ambitious project collapsed and the extension was abandoned in 1899. The Clayton West branch remained single-track and never did earn much money for its owners. British Railways converted it to DMU operation in November 1959 and it managed to soldier on for another twenty-four years, closing in 1983.

The final branch in the Huddersfield area was the longest of all four branches at 4½ miles (7.2km) and was built by the L&NWR. It left the Colne Valley main line between Hillhouse and Bradley, curving sharply away to climb through the Huddersfield outer suburbs at 1 in 66, and then following more rural surroundings, passing through Kirkheaton, Fenay Bridge and Lepton, and terminating at Kirkburton. The opening was delayed by a partial collapse of the Whitacre Mill Viaduct into the Ramsden Canal on 15 February 1866. This delayed the opening until 7 October 1867.

The line was originally intended to be a through route to Barnsley and the coal. Enough land was taken to allow for two tracks, but only one was laid. Construction started at Deighton on 10 March 1865, with the laying of contractor's sidings. Eckersley and Bayliss were the main contactors, with sub-contractors Sigley, Miles and Haynes for the viaducts and Fawcett and Son for the buildings. Construction was heavy going and included two very deep cuttings at Fenay Bridge Station. About half a million cubic yards of earth was excavated from here and used to construct the embankments on other parts of the line. A significant area of land was acquired between Kirkheaton Station and the Wakefield Road Bridge. This was for the construction of a goods yard had the line been extended.

This was another line that, not unsurprisingly, didn't provide much reward for its owners. Passenger trains ceased operation on 26 July 1930 and freight from 5 April 1965. The track was lifted in 1966. (A 1-mile section between Kirkburton Junction and Whitacre Mill Viaduct, was kept open to provide a rail connection to the ICI Chemical works. This section was closed in February 1971.)

141

Abbreviations

ABB	Asea Brown Boveri	L&NWR	London and North Western Railway
B&DJR	Birmingham and Derby Junction Railway	MCR	Midland Counties Railway
BREL	British Rail Engineering Limited	MH&R	Morecambe Harbour and Railway Company
D&D	Dearne and Dove	M&LR	Manchester and Leeds Railway
ECML	East Coast Mainline	MS&LR	Manchester, Sheffield and Lincolnshire Railway
GCR	Great Central Railway		
GER	Great Eastern Railway	MR	Midland Railway
GNER	Great North of England Railway	NER	North Eastern Railway
GNR	Great Northern Railway	NMR	North Midland Railway
H&MRCC	Huddersfield and Manchester Railway and Canal Company	NWR	North Western Railway
H&SJR	Huddersfield and Sheffield Junction Railway	SA&MR	Sheffield, Ashton-under-Lyne and Manchester Railway
H&SR	Hull and Selby Railway	SDR	Sheffield District Railway
L&BER	Leeds and Bradford Extension Railway	SRBWH&GR	Sheffield, Rotherham, Barnsley, Wakefield, Huddersfield and Goole Railway
LB&HJR	Leeds, Bradford and Halifax Junction Railway	S&RR	Sheffield and Rotherham Railway
L&BR	Leeds and Bradford Railway	SYD&GR	South Yorkshire, Doncaster and Goole Railway Company
LHBC	Lambton, Hetton and Joicey Collieries	SYR	South Yorkshire Railway
LD&ECR	Lancashire, Derbyshire and East Coast Railway	SYR&RDCo.	South Yorkshire Railway and River Don Company
L&YR	Lancashire and Yorkshire Railway	WP&GR	Wakefield, Pontefract and Goole Railway
LD&M	Leeds, Dewsbury and Manchester Railway	WR&GR	West Riding and Grimsby Railway
L&L Canal	Leeds and Liverpool Canal	WRUR	West Riding Union Railway
L&MR	Liverpool and Manchester Railway	WYPTE	West Yorkshire Passenger Transport Executive
L&SR	Leeds and Selby Railway Company	YN&BR	York, Newcastle and Berwick Railway
LMSR	London, Midland and Scottish Railway	Y&NMR	York and North Midland Railway
LNER	London and North Eastern Railway		

Index

abbreviations 142
Aire and Calder Navigation 16
Aire and Calder watershed, the 96–111
Airedale 84–92

Barnsley 66–73
    local authority commitment to rail 73
    map of railways around 70
    old 66
Beeston New Colliery 17
Bessemer, Henry 75
Bradford 96, 97
    canal 97, 98
    map of railways around 102
Bradford and Thornton Railway 107, 109–11
Brandling, Charles 16
British Rail Engineering Limited 48
buffers 105

Calder Valley, the 112–31
canal traffic delays 9
canals, the coming of 8–11
Chartists, the 128
coal, demand for 71–3
Coalfield, the 67
competition between railways 77–9
conflict and upheaval 23–4

Dewsbury 127–9
    market 128
    passenger stations 128
Doncaster 58–65

as a communication hub 58–9
early 58
station 64–5

Edmondson, Thomas 114
    card tickets 114

fire, Summit Tunnel 122–4

Great North of England Railway 44–6
Great North Road 59
Great Northern Railway 32, 60–62, 78
Grimsby 62–4

Halifax 129–31
Halifax and Ovenden Junction Railway 107
Halifax High Level Railway 107
Halifax, early history 129
Halifax, Thornton and Keighley Railway 107
Harrison, Thomas Elliot 53
Huddersfield 132–41
    origins of 133
Huddersfield and Manchester Railway and Canal Company 134
Huddersfield and Sheffield Junction Railway 118, 139–41
Huddersfield Broad Canal 9
Huddersfield Narrow Canal 9
Hudson, George 13, 23, 44, 60
Huntsman, Benjamin 75

Ingleton branch 22–3
inland transport 7–8
introduction 6–15

Kirkgate station 125
Kitson and Company 25

Lancashire and Yorkshire Railway 32, 134
Leeds and Hull Railway Company 12
Leeds and Liverpool Canal 8–9
Leeds and Selby Railway 17, 18, 19, 20
Leeds and Thirsk Railway 26
Leeds Northern Railway 30
Leeds, Bradford and Halifax Junction Railway 131
Leeds, Dewsbury and Manchester Railway 99
Leeds, map of in 1913 30
Leeds, railways around 16–37
Liverpool and Manchester Railway 11, 13, 25
London and North Western Railway 32, 86, 87
London Midland and Scottish Railway 30

Manchester and Leeds Railway 118–22
Manchester, Sheffield and Lincolnshire Railway 134
Meltham Mills Halt 140
Middleton railway 17
Midland Railway 26, 27, 32, 35, 37, 60

INDEX

navigable waterways 10
Nicholson Tunnel 136
North Eastern Railway 32
North Midland Railway 115
North Sea docks, the 62–4

Old Barnsley 66
Old Park Silver Mills 75

passenger stations 68–71
passenger-carrying railways 17–23
Plant, The 64

Queensbury lines, the 107–9

railway age begins 11–12
railway battlefield, a 6–7
railway competition 77–9
railways around Leeds 16–37
Ramsden, Sir John 133
rivers of Yorkshire 7
Rochdale Canal 9, 112, 113
Rocket, the 12
Rotherham 74–83

Settle and Carlisle Railway 89
Sheffield 74–83
   a short history of 74–5

giant marshalling yard 79–83
map of railways around 83
transport systems 76–7
South Yorkshire Coalfield 59, 66–73
Standedge Tunnel 9, 133, 137
   tunnelling delays at 133
Stephenson, George 12, 14, 23, 44
Stephenson, Robert 12
Stockton and Darling Railway Company 10
Summit Tunnel fire 122–4

Titfield Thunderbolt, The 25
trade, establishment of 7
traffic delays, canal 9
tramroads, the first 67–8
transport, need for inland 7–8

Wakefield 124–7
Wakefield, Pontefract and Goole Railway 60
water highways 67
waterway dividends 12
waterways map 10
West Riding
   history of 6–15
   navigable waterways of 10

railways, map of in 1845 15
West Riding Union Railway 26
West Yorkshire Passenger Transport Executive 95
Wharfedale 92–5
Woodhead Tunnel 77, 136, 137
wool barons 90

York 38–57
   confectionery 57
   industrial revolution 42–3
   medieval 39–40
   railways come to 44–8
   revival prior to industrial revolution 40–42
   Roman 38–9
   trade 43–4
York and North Midland Railway 46, 49–57
York, Newcastle and Berwick Railway 30
Yorkshire Coalfield 59
Yorkshire rivers 7
Yorkshire wagonways 16–17